Merr

2013

AMAZING & EXTRAORDINARY FACTS

J.R.R. TOLKIEN

AMAZING & EXTRAORDINARY FACTS

J.R.R. TOLKIEN

COLIN DURIEZ

David and Charles

Dedication

In memory of my dear sister
Barbara Pauline Duriez
23 March 1945 to 30 January 2007

CONTENTS

INTRODUCTION

Hobbits are said to love tobacco, ordinary humdrum life, locally brewed beer, and colourful waistcoats. So too did their creator, who once described himself as in essence a Hobbit in all but size.

Though undoubtedly an academic (and perhaps a hobbit), there was much more to J.R.R. Tolkien. He was kidnapped (or rather, borrowed without permission) as a baby in South Africa, orphaned, survived the bloody Battle of the Somme of World War One with deep mental scars, and preferred ordinary family life and seaside holidays to his later celebrity. His major book, *The Lord of the Rings*, one of the most popular and successful stories of our time, was expected by its doubting publisher to make a big loss.

The 'Hobbit man' is hard to sum up, even going by statements he made about himself. I put together this collection of fascinating and intriguing facts about the creator of Hobbits just after writing about his life. In that biography, as you might expect, I tried to capture his often cryptic personality, so as to provide a rounded and accurate portrait. In compiling this present book, I've discovered that selecting representative facts about the scholar and storyteller, and arranging them thematically, unexpectedly results in a mosaic portrait that adds a new dimension to understanding his life.

Why such a compilation of facts does so is not easy to discover. It is, I think, because Tolkien is full of apparent contrasts and even paradoxes. He has of course become one of the most famous storytellers in the world. In the arcane world of literary and linguistic scholarship, however, he was also an outstanding figure. He gained his first university Chair in English language at the youthful age of 32 at Leeds and, the following year, he moved to Oxford University as Professor of Anglo-Saxon. A fundamentally shy and deeply reflective person, he in fact thrived on friendship and often hearty companionship. At a time when fantasy, and fairy-tale in particular, was consigned to childhood, he championed such wonder tales as adult fare, and succeeded in creating a genre for grown-ups that is evident in bookshops throughout the world.

In this book you may happily flit here and there, perhaps from ordinary places like Warwick or Birmingham that inspired Tolkien to imaginary creatures or settings, or from his world of scholarship to the faith that sustained him but, wherever you go, you will be certain to find clues and insights that throw light upon Tolkien, and also upon his creation of Middle-earth that has cast its spell around the planet.

Behind the person and his remarkably detailed imaginative world of Hobbits and Elves are ideas as startling as those explored by the best of science-fiction writers and visionary thinkers. But, in yet another paradox, Tolkien's inspiration mainly centres upon a nearly lost past world which turns out to be remarkably applicable to our modern lives and dilemmas. In his lifetime he could be, and often was, dismissed as a fuddy-duddy scholar of ancient words and languages, and writer of out-of-touch fiction. Today, the chords his ideas, beliefs and interests have struck around the world make such a dismissal very much harder. He now appears much more mainstream than at the backwaters in the currents of our time. Tolkien was an amazing and extraordinary person in himself – and that's the biggest fact in this book.

Colin Duriez

J.R.R. TOLKIEN, THE MAN BEHIND MIDDLE-EARTH

Was Tolkien a spy?
The Bletchley connection

'J.R.R. Tolkien trained as British spy,' screamed a headline in *The Daily Telegraph*. The newspaper was reporting on an exhibition held in 2009 at G.C.H.Q, the British government's intelligence centre in Gloucestershire, which revealed hitherto secret information. Although Tolkien was never on his way to becoming an eccentric spy, the real truth is interesting – and has a connection to Bletchley, the famous intelligence centre.

In the months prior to the outbreak of the Second World War, Tolkien agreed to work for the Foreign Office decoding encrypted messages; he did some brief initial training to provide him with a taste of what would be required. At this time, there was a possibility that he could have ended up working at Bletchley Park in Buckinghamshire. This was famously where academics, mathematicians and early computer wizards such as Alan Turing eventually broke the Nazi's Enigma code; much else was achieved there, too.

Yet for some reason the authorities decided, soon after the war broke out in September 1939, that Tolkien's cryptographical services were not required. It is possible that personal factors influenced their decision: Tolkien had suffered concussion in the summer of 1939, which affected his health for a time; his wife Edith had been ill; in addition, Tolkien had effectively become head of his university department due to wartime staff shortages, thereby increasing his administrative burdens.

A number of leading academics

Bletchley Park, Buckinghamshire

with suitable skills, it seems, had been head hunted over the years as candidates for busting code, Tolkien among them. Indeed, in the First World War he had hands-on experience with signals in trench warfare, and undertook training in communications. This, combined with his formidable linguistic knowledge, may have made Tolkien initially attractive to the intelligence services.

The Dead Marshes
Tolkien and the Battle of the Somme

J. R. R. Tolkien, 1916

In 1916 – the year that J.R.R. Tolkien married Edith Bratt – he served from July to October in the Battle of the Somme, one of the bloodiest episodes of the First World War. The battle took place where the armies' front lines crossed the valley of the River Somme in France. Tolkien's battalion – the 11th Lancashire Fusiliers – fought in rural places that have entered history, such as Ovillers-la-Boisselle and Thiepval Wood, as well as other locations named by soldiers, such as the strategic Schwaben Redoubt, a German stronghold.

As the battle drew to a close, Tolkien was evacuated to England suffering from severe trench fever. 'Rob' Gilson, Tolkien's good friend, had been killed on the very first day of the Battle. A second friend, Geoffrey Smith, died soon after it ended when, some days after being wounded by shrapnel, a deadly gangrene had set in. The total Allied gain during the battle was only about 8 miles (13km), yet had cost approximately 615,000 Allied and 500,000 German casualties.

At that time, Tolkien was in the early stages of creating what would become his mythology of Middle-earth. Yet, while he was in the trenches Tolkien didn't write stories or verse, as some have thought: 'That's all spoof,' he told an interviewer. The most he could do was to scribble some words on the back of an envelope as he, like his fellow soldiers, were huddled down 'among flies and filth' in the chill autumn mud.

The memories of modern warfare would haunt his later writings, as seen in 'The Passage of the Marshes', a chapter from *The Lord of the Rings*. Here we read of Sam Gamgee the Hobbit tripping as he hurries forward, his hand sinking into the marsh. Seeing dead faces in the water, he cries out and springs back in horror. Gollum laughs at his reaction, and then explains the meaning behind the name of the Dead Marshes. Sam and Frodo understand from him that there had been a great battle in that place long ago, in which men and Elves had fallen in great numbers.

For Tolkien, those long dead faces staring up from under the water could have included his fallen friends, such as 'Rob' Gilson. Indeed, the loss of close friends in battle was a strong motivation for Tolkien to write his mythology, in order to make some sense of the aspirations he had shared with them. He later observed: 'A real taste for fairy-stories was…quickened to full life by war.'

TRENCH FEVER

In the foul conditions of the wartime trenches, body lice were rife; trench fever was caused by an infection that these pests carried. Symptoms included a fever, headaches, soreness in bones, joints and muscles, and lesions of the skin on the back and chest. Most of those afflicted recovered within about two months, but the fever became more serious in around 5 per cent of cases. Indeed, Tolkien's infection was acute enough to require his return to England and hospitalisation. Trench fever was first officially identified in 1915, as a result of the condition found among the troops of the First World War.

Birmingham
Tolkien's home city

J.R.R Tolkien regarded the city of his childhood, Birmingham in England, as his home city. Then, as now, it was one of Britain's major urban sprawls, yet it was naturally far smaller then than it is today. Indeed, many of the places Tolkien remembered with affection were then just villages or small towns in the deeply rural surround of the city boundaries.

John Ronald Reuel Tolkien was born on 3 January 1892. At the time of his father's death in South Africa in 1896, the four-year-old Ronald Tolkien and his brother, Hilary, were in England with their mother, Mabel, because of the young Tolkien's health. They remained in England after his father's death, and occupied a rented house in Sarehole, Warwickshire — an area outside Birmingham — close to Sarehole Mill.

King Edward's School, Birmingham

Tolkien attended King Edward's School, at the time located in Birmingham city centre. For much of his school life he and Hilary lived in nearby Edgbaston, first with Mabel, and then, after she died of diabetes, as orphans under the guardianship of a genial priest from the neighbouring Birmingham Oratory. With a group of friends from a schoolboy club, Tolkien met and supped tea at Barrow's Stores in Corporation Street, near the school.

Birmingham had gained city status in 1889, and was famous internationally for its manufacturing. The Industrial Revolution had begun in nearby Ironbridge and Birmingham's metal industries had

been important since the last half of the seventeenth century. Today, the city's famous author has been honoured by the establishment of The Shire Country Park, and the preservation of Sarehole Mill, the latter of course also preserved because of its association with Matthew Boulton and the Industrial Revolution.

KING EDWARD'S SCHOOL

Tolkien studied at King Edward's School, which was Birmingham's top grammar school. The all-boys' school was then located beside New Street Station, and the school's buildings – since demolished – bore the mark of their architect, Sir Charles Barry, who also designed the current Houses of Parliament in London. It was at King Edward's School that Tolkien received a thorough grounding in the classics, was introduced to Middle English, and was prepared for entrance to Oxford University. He also forged close friendships in a schoolboy coterie, which endured into his early adulthood.

The real Two Towers?
Edgbaston's landmark towers

The skyline of Edgbaston in Birmingham is dominated in places by two towers: one a notable monument to industrial utility; the other a graceful memorial to an eighteenth-century aristocrat. The former is the chimney of the local Victorian waterworks; the latter is an eighteenth-century tower named Perrott's Folly, after its maker, John Perrott, and was built next to what had been his lodge, where there was once an enclosed hunting park. Tolkien lived at various addresses in Edgbaston between 1902 and 1911, so was familiar with both looming towers nearby. Indeed, the 'two towers' is the local name for the edifices, and speculation

Waterworks, Edgbaston

is that they inspired Tolkien's *The Lord of the Rings*. Of course the middle volume of the trilogy is even entitled *The Two Towers*.

The idea that the Edgbaston towers inspired Tolkien is an attractive one. What complicates it, however, is identifying the two Middle-earth towers to which the title, *The Two Towers*, refers. Even Tolkien himself gave conflicting messages about their identity. Were they Minas Morgul, the city fortress Frodo Baggins encounters on his approach to Mordor, and Minas Tirith, the city of Gondor, as local people speculate? Alternatively, were they Orthanc, Saruman's tower, and Barad-dûr, Sauron's Dark Tower? Or were they even Orthanc and the Tower of Cirith Ungol, where Frodo is taken as a captive at the end of *The Two Towers*? Tolkien seems to have inclined towards the latter combination, but recognizes a basic opposition in the story between Minas Tirith, the focus of the strength of the Western allies, and Sauron's Dark Tower, Barad-dûr. Intriguingly, in his final cover design for *The Two Towers* he draws Minas Morgoth and Orthanc.

WATERWORKS TOWER

During Tolkien's years in Edgbaston he lived for a while close to the Waterworks, the site of ceaseless activity. The Waterworks' elaborate chimney towered above its engine room, boiler house and workshops; sometimes, like Saruman's devilish workings around Orthanc, it would thrust out black smoke to the sound of rhythmic pumps. Shockwaves from these pumps pulsated through the ground for a fair distance as the good folk of Birmingham and Aston were supplied with water from bore holes. The Waterworks Tower might have played a part in providing the inspiration for Orthanc, although it does not resemble Saruman's tower.

J.R.R. Tolkien in fiction
Some remarkable portrayals

J.R.R. Tolkien outwardly led an unremarkable life: he was a family man who liked seaside holidays and daytrips into the countryside; his professional life was spent mainly in academic work, first at Leeds and then at Oxford universities; one of his favourite pastimes was to meet with friends, in pubs or in college rooms. Yet surprisingly, he presents a remarkably attractive figure for the writer of fiction. Although the portrayals of Tolkien in fiction, by the author himself and others, add nothing to our factual knowledge of the man, they do add to our understanding and affect how we see him.

'Leaf by Niggle' is a story by Tolkien, which is unusual for containing elements drawn from his own life. It is an allegory, also unusual for Tolkien, where places and characters in the story correspond directly to ideas. The allegorical elements can be interpreted in great detail: the character Niggle, for instance, knows that one day he will have to make a journey that, allegorically, stands for death. Furthermore, Niggle is a painter and as such represents Tolkien, the niggling writer.

The Lost Road is a story that Tolkien never finished. He began writing this shortly after he was challenged by C.S. Lewis to write a tale for adults about time travel. The story explores the concept of an unusual father-and-son relationship repeated at various times in history, as discovered by the contemporary father and son as they travel through ancestral memory. The character of Alboin particularly resembles Tolkien, being born around the same time as the author. In the story, the character illuminates the creative process of discovery that led Tolkien to write *The Silmarillion* material, and eventually *The Lord of the Rings*.

During the period Tolkien was writing *The Lost Road*, C.S. Lewis was working on his own story of space travel entitled *Out of the Silent Planet* (1938). Lewis's story includes a character who somewhat resembles Tolkien, named Elwin Ransom. The meaning of Elwin is 'Elf-friend' and Ransom, in the story, is a Cambridge philologist possessed by a love of language.

Young Pattullo (1975) is the second in a series of five novels by J.I.M. Stewart, collectively entitled *A Staircase in Surrey* (1974–1978). It follows events as the leading character, Duncan Pattullo, begins his studies at Oxford. One of his tutors owes much to Tolkien: Dr J.B. Timbermill, M.A., D. Litt, F.B.A., is a fellow, like Tolkien, of Merton College. His tutorials are held in Timbermill's home in north Oxford, an area where Tolkien lived. The third novel in the series entitled *A Memorial Service* (1976) sees Pattulo return to Oxford in his middle-age years to take up a fellowship in his old college, and fills out the picture of Timbermill, the elusive philological scholar, who writes a fantasy called *The Magic Quest* that makes him famous.

HEAVEN'S WAR
Written by Micah Harris and illustrated by Michael Gaydos, Heaven's War (2003) is a fantasy graphic novel about Tolkien and his fellow Inklings, C. S. Lewis and Charles Williams. In 1938, as global war becomes increasingly likely, the three are drawn into battle against supernatural forces associated with the occult and led by Aleister Crowley, also an actual person. The arcane twists and turns of the plot are at times reminiscent of both Dan Brown's The Da Vinci Code and Charles Williams' supernatural novels.

'I am...a Hobbit'
How J.R.R. Tolkien saw himself

J.R.R. Tolkien was to capture the world of his childhood in his portrayal of The Shire in *The Hobbit* and *The Lord of the Rings*. In fact, in a letter he wrote of living his early years 'in "The Shire" in a pre-mechanical age'. He saw himself, no doubt with a twinkle in his eye, as a Hobbit: in that same letter, he went on to say that he was a Hobbit in fact, although not in size. Like Hobbits, he explained, he relished gardens, trees and farmlands that were not mechanized. He, too, liked his food plain, had a fondness for eating mushrooms straight from the field, and smoked a pipe. In the drab mid-twentieth century, Tolkien enjoyed wearing ornamental waistcoats and liked exercising his very basic sense of humour, which some found tiresome. He added that he went to bed late and, if possible, got up late. Also like Hobbits, he was little travelled.

Of the Hobbits he created, Tolkien perhaps most resembles Mr Bilbo Baggins, who we first meet in *The Hobbit*. On the surface Bilbo

Aftermath of the storm, 1987

appears bourgeois, the stereotype of a middle-class gentleman. But as it turns out, there is far more to him than meets the eye. Bilbo is undoubtedly one of the most scholarly of the Hobbits, being a main contributor to the *Red Book* – named after its red leather binding – which is written by Hobbits and chronicles the events of *The Hobbit* and *The Lord of the Rings*. Attached to the *Red Book* are a number of other chronicles, including the three volumes of Bilbo's translations from Elvish of the material concerning the early ages of Middle-earth preceding the period of *The Lord of the Rings*. As translations, these retain the high 'Elvish' style that makes *The Silmarillion* so different from *The Hobbit* and *The Lord of the Rings*.

A remarkable coincidence
Did J.R.R Tolkien predict the great storm of 1987?

Not long after the Second World War, J.R.R. Tolkien started writing a new story, *The Notion Club Papers*, while still working upon his unfinished manuscript, *The Lord of the Rings*. In this new story, he told of a great storm that raged over the Midlands and southern England during the night of 12 June 1987. The storm was the fiercest in living memory, flattening acres of trees in woodland, parks and forests as it hurtled across countryside and urban areas. Houses and hotels collapsed, roads and railway lines were blocked by thousands of trees, and the storm left in its wake a swath of damage from Cornwall to East Anglia.

Tolkien wrote of a club of like-minded academics, called the Notion Club, who met in the rooms of Michael Ramer, Professor of Finno-Ugric Philology, in Jesus College, Oxford. In the story, they discuss their exploration of dreams, words and phrases that were helping them to build a picture of an ancient disaster that had swallowed an island kingdom deep in the Atlantic. It transpired that this island was named Númenor, the island from Tolkien's world of Middle-earth.

This group of academics bore some remarkable similarities to the Inklings, the cluster of friends to which Tolkien belonged in the real world. Indeed, Tolkien was to read his fictional account of a great storm and a literary club, set in the future world of 1987, to some of the Inklings in the summer of 1946. Moreover, by remarkable coincidence he was only about four months out in his timing of a great storm; in reality, the storm of the century was actually to strike England late on 15 October 1987.

In the story, the great force responsible for the storm that blasted late twentieth-century Oxford issued from the calamity that had befallen Númenor many thousands of years before. This was as a direct consequence of the time link made by members of the Notion Club as they explored the ancient past through traces of forgotten languages and persistent dreams.

THE NOTION CLUB PAPERS

The Notion Club Papers *is an incomplete story written by Tolkien between 1945 and 1946. Set in the future, it comprises the fictional notes of meetings held by the Notion Club in Oxford between 1986 and 1987, supposedly discovered early in the twenty-first century. Tolkien intended this story of time travel to introduce Númenor, the island whose tale was eventually told in* **The Silmarillion.** *Meetings of the Inklings in the immediate post-war period provided Tolkien with inspiration for the informal literary group in his story; the fictional academics in the Notion Club resemble in some ways real*

*members of the more diverse circle of
Inklings to which Tolkien belonged.*

In the company
of friends
Favoured pubs and eating places

J.R.R. Tolkien frequented a
number of public houses in
Oxford, in the company of friends.
We know about some of his visits
to these houses with members
of the Inklings, in particular.
Occasionally these friends would
also eat together in a hotel
restaurant, rather than in a college.

For many years, the Eagle and
Child, familiarly known as 'The Bird
and Baby', was a popular meeting
place for the literary group. From
1939 to (around) 1962, various
members of the Inklings would
gather at the pub, often on a Tuesday
morning. Tolkien attended many
of these meetings, particularly up
until the early 1950s. Fascinatingly,
the pub's sign shows an image of
the divine mortal Ganymede being
abducted by Zeus in the form of an
eagle; the establishment stands in St

Giles, opposite another favoured pub,
the Lamb and Flag. In addition, other
pubs frequented at times by Tolkien
and friends include the Kings Arms,
near the Bodleian Library, and the
White Horse nearby, a very small pub
full of character and situated next to
Blackwell's bookshop.

One of the places favoured at various
times by Tolkien and his friends for
eating as well as for drinking was the
Eastgate Hotel on the High Street. After
the death of his wife Edith, Tolkien
was living in Merton Street, only a few
doors away, and he often visited the
hotel. Indeed, for many years, he would
meet C.S. Lewis on Monday mornings
in his friend's rooms at Magdalen
College, then the two would have a
drink at the Eastgate, which was not
far away. Another popular hotel for its
bar or for a meal was the Mitre, also
on High Street; originally established
around 1300, this is one of the oldest
inns in Oxford. After staying at the
Mitre in the 1950s, the science-fiction
writer Arthur C. Clarke wrote of it as
'a wonderful, non-Euclidian building
with no right angles in it, no two rooms
the same'.

PUBS IN THE SHIRE

*The traditional English pub is
a setting that forms part of the
ordinary life loved by J.R.R. Tolkien.
In **The Lord of the Rings**, similar
pubs are associated with The Shire of
the Hobbits and with Bree, a town
east of The Shire visited by Hobbits.
Hobbiton itself has a small inn on
the Bywater road called the Ivy Bush.
The Hobbit Pippin makes reference
to the Golden Perch at the village of
Stock that, in his opinion, has the
finest beer in the Eastfarthing. And at
Bree, Frodo and his companions stay
at The Prancing Pony, run by the
forgetful Barliman Butterbur.*

PLACES, REAL AND IMAGINED

J.R.R. Tolkien's universe
The cosmos of Middle-earth

The Middle-earth of J.R.R.
Tolkien's stories is in many
respects intended to physically
resemble our own world. This is
especially the case with its landscape;
for example The Shire, the Misty
Mountains, and the long river basin
of the Anduin – along which Frodo
Baggins and his companions travel in
their quest – all echo the geography
of ancient northwest Europe. It is
with respect to time that Tolkien's
stories diverge to offer a form of
alternative history; the events of the
War of the Ring, for instance, suggest
an alternative history set many
thousands of years ago.

It is because of this geographical
symmetry that the night sky of
Middle-earth resembles that which
we see today, and our ancestors saw
thousands of years ago. For example,
the star of Eärendil in the sky of
Tolkien's Middle-earth corresponds
to the bright planet Venus – or
the Evening and Morning Star –

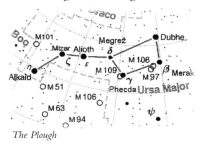

The Plough

of our own night sky. The deity Varda, one of the Valar or angelic guardians of the world, placed the Seven Stars – or the Sickle of the Valar – in the sky of Middle-earth to precipitate the awakening of the Elves and the ultimate defeat of the satanic Morgoth. These Seven Stars correspond to the Plough, or the Great Bear, of our own sky. Other counterparts between the skies of Middle-earth and our own include:

CARNIL: MARS
LUINIL: NEPTUNE
NÉNAR: URANUS
LUMBAR: SATURN
ALCARINQUË: JUPITER
ELLEMÍRË: MERCURY

The cosmos of Tolkien's invented world is mainly associated with the deity Varda, the most beloved of the Valar, or angelic powers, of Middle-earth. Her popular name is Elbereth, meaning 'star-queen'; she is also known as Snow-white. Varda set the stars alight and dwelt with Manwë, her husband, on Mount Taniquetil, whose peak rose into the stars. Varda is particularly associated with light,

which is a central theme in the stories of Middle-earth. She set the star Eärendil in the sky, and helped Sam Gamgee the Hobbit use the Phial of Galadriel when he found himself in the lair of the monstrous spider, Shelob, in *The Lord of the Rings*.

Tolkien's early universe is the stuff of myth rather than actual geography, with a flat world. It is only after the destruction of the star-shaped island of Númenor that the earth becomes a globe, and various realms of the blessed become separated from Middle-earth. Then, the Undying Lands of the utter West – Valinor – can only be reached by the Straight Road, the way taken by Frodo, Bilbo and the three keepers of the Elven Rings when they set sail from the Grey Havens at the end of *The Lord of the Rings*. Tolkien never completed the scheme of his astronomy to fully harmonize the early mythic and the later, more realistic, cosmos, yet he always attempted to retain some physical resemblance between the real and his invented world.

The real Bag End, Worcestershire

EÄRENDIL: THE STAR THAT INSPIRED MIDDLE-EARTH

Eärendil is the mariner who intercedes on behalf of the Elves and men of Middle-earth when in distress from the evil of Morgoth. After this, he 'sailed out of the mists of the world into the seas of heaven with the Silmaril upon his brow'. His star in the sky was a sign of the providence of Ilúvatar, the maker of all, and provided hope to the faithful. The name 'Earendel' in the Old English poem **Christ** *was an important seed for the growth of Tolkien's invented mythology; the story of this character's life and voyage is one of its earliest elements.*

The real Bag End
Origins of a Hobbit hole

J.R.R. Tolkien had a favourite aunt, Jane Neave, who was the younger sister of his mother, Mabel; she was to become an important figure in Tolkien's life. With a B.Sc. degree in geology, botany and physiology, Jane became a professional woman, a rare achievement in her day. Amongst other jobs she managed farms: first Phoenix Farm near Nottingham, and then Bag End in Dormston, close to Inkberrow, in Worcestershire.

People in the area at some stage called the latter farm Bag End, and it is thus marked on old maps. Its location at the end of a lane gave rise to its name, which is a straightforward translation of the adopted French term 'cul de sac'. The farm was an old, rather dilapidated manor house and Tolkien often visited his aunt there. Today what was once the farm is now a house called Dormston Manor.

Of course in *The Hobbit* and *The Lord of the Rings*, Bag End is the name of Bilbo Baggins's comfortable Hobbit hole, which is eventually inherited by Frodo Baggins. The setting of Bag End farm in Worcestershire, a county that was to become a major source of inspiration for Tolkien's The Shire, only serves to heighten the sense that Bag End farm almost belonged to the author's invented world.

A TASTE OF THE SHIRE
Today Bag End farm is a private house. It remains at the end of a lane, and is still surrounded by fields. Its rural setting provides a tantalizing and eloquent taste of Tolkien's Shire.

Sarehole Mill

Where is The Shire?
A strangely familiar place

One will find many landscapes in northwest Europe which resemble J.R.R. Tolkien's invented Shire, the home of the Hobbits at the time of events in *The Hobbit* and *The Lord of the Rings*; it was certainly the author's intention for these stories to evoke a sense of familiarity in their geography. Yet Tolkien's Shire was based on very specific locations: namely rural Worcestershire and Warwickshire, and the neighbouring counties of the historic West Midlands – Herefordshire, Shropshire and Staffordshire. Even more specifically than the West Midlands area, the heart of The Shire's 'Englishness' was based upon a tiny village that remained at the time deeply rustic, despite its location close to the boundaries of late nineteenth-century Birmingham.

After the death of his father, Tolkien's mother rented a house in Sarehole village for herself and her two young boys. Nearby was Sarehole Mill, run by a father and son. The large brick building was powered by a steam engine that supplemented the stream that powered its great wheel. Hobbiton, home of Bilbo Baggins and other Hobbits like Sam Gamgee and Bilbo's nephew Frodo, is partly based on Sarehill. In a letter written nearly 60 years after his few years spent in the quiet village, Tolkien revealed a 'significant' fact about himself: 'I…lived for my early years in "the Shire" in a pre-mechanical age.' Moreover, in a letter to his publisher he specified that The Shire was 'more or less a Warwickshire village of about the period of the Diamond Jubilee', of Queen Victoria in 1897.

Hilary, Tolkien's younger brother, wrote a few story fragments about the idyllic times the family spent in Sarehole, also capturing in them the terror felt by the two brothers for the miller's son and an old farmer from nearby Sarehole Farm who once chased Tolkien for picking mushrooms. In his stories, Hilary called the Sarehole area 'Ogre Country', with the old farmer featuring as the Black Ogre and the miller's son as the White Ogre. Edited by Angela Gardner and illustrated by Jef Murray, the stories are published in *Black and White Ogre Country: The Lost Tales of Hilary Tolkien* (2009). Tolkien himself wrote of the old miller and his son as 'characters of wonder and terror to a small child'.

TOLKIEN'S WEST MIDLANDS

J.R.R. Tolkien considered the West Midlands his home. His mother was born Mabel Suffield, from a family long associated with the West Midlands, in particular Evesham in Worcestershire. He was emotionally attached to his Suffield ancestry, which tied him to the West Midland region that was to him The Shire of his stories. As well as an inspiration for his fiction, this attachment gave him a fervent interest in the dialect of the region and the examples of its literature that had survived. Furthermore, much of his scholarly interest centred on the English language and literature of the West Midlands, especially that written in the fourteenth century.

A holiday in the Swiss Alps
Making its mark upon The Hobbit

Jungfrau, Switzerland

During the summer of 1911, just before he began his university studies in Oxford, J.R.R. Tolkien visited Switzerland on holiday with his younger brother, Hilary. They were members of a party of adults and children that included Tolkien's aunt Jane Neave, as well as female schoolteachers and a family with which Jane was friendly. All were equipped with tall walking staffs, sturdy footwear and wide-brimmed hats as they were taking part in an ambitious walking holiday that was to culminate in a trek up the vast Aletsch glacier. Much of the time the group followed mountain tracks, and sometimes slept rough in barns.

The teeming repository of remembered places and events that Tolkien brought back with him from Switzerland were to transform themselves into stories and locations of his invented Middle-earth. The party made its way past the giant peaks of the Eiger, the Mönch, and the Jungfrau, which inspired Tolkien's receptive imagination, thus appearing in his drawings and descriptions of the Misty Mountains in *The Hobbit* and *The Lord of the Rings*. In addition, the sheer sides of the Lauterbrunnen valley may well have planted the seeds of inspiration for Tolkien's Rivendell.

Guides accompanied the holidaymakers when they came to experience the challenges of the Aletsch glacier. That year, there had been months of hot weather; boulders and stones that were normally gripped securely by the ice were exposed and becoming loose. Tolkien confessed that he 'came near to perishing'. As they plodded along a narrow track on a steep, snowy slope, rocks above them began tumbling down. One passed between Tolkien and an elderly teacher in front of him. She leapt out of its path; the boulder missed Tolkien by a mere foot.

The incident helped inspire the 'thunderbattle' in Chapter 4 of *The Hobbit,* which drives Bilbo Baggins, Thorin's company of dwarves and the wizard Gandalf to shelter in a cave. It possibly also inspired Tolkien's drawing of 'The Mountain-path' from the same chapter.

The Lonely Isle
Tol Eressëa, a legendary England

The large, isolated island of Tol Eressëa is one of the earliest locations created by Tolkien as he shaped the world of Middle-earth. Before the sun and the moon shone in the sky, its western shore received the light of the Two Trees from Valinor, the realm of the Valar or angelic powers. Many Elves eventually settled on the green island of Tol Eressëa, building the white harbour and city of Avallónë. Lamps lit its quays, and the island's beautiful white tower could be seen from vast distances away. The island's name is Elvish for 'Lonely Isle', which reflects its isolation from the great landmass on which the humans and other races lived.

In Tolkien's earliest version of his history of Middle-earth entitled *The Book of Lost Tales*, he conceived and presented Tol Eressëa as a mythical equivalent of England, but one inhabited by Elves. In the *Lost Tales*, Aelfwine, an ancient British mariner, discovers the Lonely Isle; there, in a Warwickshire-like setting, he discovers the Cottage of Lost Play where he is told early versions of the mythological stories that eventually appear in *The Silmarillion*.

Like The Shire, the original Tol Eressëa is a homely place that Tolkien closely associates with his childhood experience of living in the West Midlands at the end of the nineteenth and the early twentieth centuries. As well as this 'homeliness' on an island scale in the form of Tol Eressëa, the

Cottage of Lost Play found there is one of many homely dwellings and places that Tolkien created in his work; others include Bag End, Crickhollow, the House of Tom Bombadil, The Prancing Pony inn, and Rivendell.

KORTIRION, OR WARWICK

Warwick is the county town of Warwickshire, situated about 20 miles (32km) from Birmingham where Tolkien spent his youth, and is the city where he courted and married his wife, Edith Bratt. In the early stages of his mythology, Warwick is represented by Kortirion, which is the principal city – complete with a tower and situated in a region of elms that represents Warwickshire – of Tol

Eressëa, which stands for England. The name 'Kortirion' is Elvish, in Tolkien's invented language perhaps meaning 'a mighty tower, a city on a hill'. Tolkien describes the city of Kortirion in some detail in an early poem entitled **Kortirion Among the Trees,** *based upon his knowledge of Warwick.*

Lydney Park Excavations
J.R.R. Tolkien and the god Nodens

In 1928 J.R.R. Tolkien, then Professor of Anglo-Saxon at Oxford, was briefly employed as consultant on an archaeological project on a slope above the Severn estuary at Lydney Park in the Forest

Warwick Castle

of Dean, Gloucestershire. Running the project was the celebrated Mortimer (later Sir Mortimer) Wheeler and his wife, Tessa Wheeler. At the fourth-century Romano-British temple on the site, an obscure and rare name 'Nodens' had been inscribed upon plates of bronze and lead. Tolkien was to extensively research this name, using his philological skills and uncanny insight into the latent history of individual words to help him.

At one time, the area was an Iron Age earthwork known as Lydney Camp. More recently, the Romans had twice exploited the 4-acre (2 hectare) site: in the first phase, they honeycombed the area with shafts for iron mining; in the second, they built a temple and adjacent bathhouse for pilgrims. What particularly intrigued the Wheelers was the religious dimension to the newer site. After the Romans, the Anglo-Saxons dubbed the area Dwarf's Hill, already providing the locality with a 'Tolkienesque' colour.

One of the aims of the project and its report, as stated by the Wheelers, was to 'examine the particular nature of the Lydney cult as witnessed… by the name of the presiding deity'. Thus as a result of his research, Tolkien wrote a learned essay on the divinity's name, which appeared as an appendix to the Wheeler report on the excavation entitled simply 'The Name "Nodens" '. In it, Tolkien concluded that Nodens is a variation of the Irish hero and god Núada of the Silver Hand, King of the Fair Folk of Irish legend, and therefore a Fairy King. Tolkien also linked the name to Welsh figures of legend, including Nudd, or Lludd. He theorized that Nodens implies an earlier deity whose name meant Snarer, or Hunter. In this research, it is fascinating to see Tolkien demonstrate his remarkable ability to draw out signs of a lost mythology from a single word.

Remains of the Roman temple, Lydney Park

Professor David Hinton, an archaeologist, and others have suggested that the excavation may have influenced Tolkien's fiction. As well as folklore about Dwarf's Hill, there was an inscription to Nodens that mentioned a valuable missing ring, large holes on a green hillside like a Hobbit settlement, Tolkien's own link from the name 'Nodens' to 'the Silver Hand' in Ireland and Wales, and an allusion to a Fairy King, to name just a few of the tantalizing possibilities. Indeed, in the final sentence of his essay, Tolkien's words reveal how much the discovery of the inscriptions of Nodens had fired his imagination: 'Even in the dimmed memories of Welsh legend in *llaw erient* we hear still an echo of the ancient fame of the magic hand of Nodens the Catcher.'

THE BARROW DOWNS

In **The Lord of the Rings** *the name of the Barrow Downs, to the east of the Old Forest, is derived from the Great Barrows, or stone-chambered burial mounds, which date back to ancient days, before men had crossed the Ered Luin – the Blue Mountains – into Beleriand. Earlier in the Third Age, evil spirits from Angmar called the barrow-wights had possessed the burial mounds, making the region an area of dread; in the story, Tom Bombadil rescues Frodo Baggins and his Hobbit companions from these barrow-wights. Tolkien and his family were familiar with the Ridgeway walk above the Vale of the White Horse, and the nearby Wayland's Smithy, a large Neolithic long barrow with burial chambers that no doubt influenced the barrow locations of his story.*

A burial chamber at Wayland's Smithy

LANGUAGES AND NAMES, REAL AND INVENTED

Anglo-Saxon
The most ancient form of English

J.R.R. Tolkien was Rawlinson and Bosworth Professor of Anglo-Saxon at Oxford University from 1926 to 1945, before transferring to another Oxford Chair as Merton Professor of English Language and Literature where he continued to teach some Anglo-Saxon until a late retirement. Teaching Anglo-Saxon had also been an important responsibility in his previous appointments at Leeds University. Indeed, the language was a life-long interest from schooldays, as well as being at the centre of his scholarship.

Anglo-Saxon, or Old English, broadly refers to the language of English people up until the Norman Conquest. The period of Anglo-Saxon literature is recognized to stretch from the Anglian invasion in the fifth and sixth centuries to the first half of the twelfth century. What

has survived is comparatively little, but includes poetry Tolkien frequently taught, such as *Beowulf, Judith, The Wanderer, Seafarer, Maldon, The Phoenix and Dream of the Rood* [Cross].

As a lecturer, Tolkien quickly discovered the effectiveness of opening a lecture with reading *Beowulf* aloud. This early English poem began with 'Hwaet!' or 'listen!' yet, to uninitiated undergraduates, it sounded like 'Quiet!' For the poet W.H. Auden as a student of the Professor, Tolkien reciting from *Beowulf* 'was the voice of Gandalf'.

Tolkien's love for Anglo-Saxon is evident throughout his fiction as well as his scholarship. His 'Middle-earth' is an old name for the world, taken from northern mythology and occurring in Old English literature. The Hobbit name for July, 'Afterlithe', is from the Old English word for the same month, 'aefterlith'; similarly, the Hobbit 'Afteryule' corresponds to January, and is from the Old English 'aefter Geola' meaning 'after Winter-Solstice'. In *The Lord of the Rings*, Tolkien uses Old English sources for the words and names of the people of Rohan.

A FRAGMENT OF HISTORY TRANSLATED

The Shaping of Middle-earth (1986) is the fourth volume of The History of Middle-earth, *the analysis of Tolkien's invented world edited and published by his son, Christopher, after Tolkien's death. In its pages, it includes the original 'Silmarillion' written by Tolkien in 1926, and the only form of the mythology of the First Age of Middle-earth that Tolkien ever completed: the 'Quenta', or history, from 1930. To that is added a fragment of the history of Middle-earth translated into Old English by Aelfwine, a mariner from the Anglo-Saxon period to whom the tales of the First Age were first told, who features in Tolkien's early fiction.*

Master of many languages
Translations and retellings by J.R.R. Tolkien

Translations and retellings played a significant role in J.R.R. Tolkien's scholarly development and in his literary devices. During his school days at King Edward's School in Birmingham, Tolkien was introduced to Anglo-Saxon or Old English, and discovered Gothic and other languages such as Finnish. As

The dragon Fafnir guarding his hoard

an undergraduate, he experimented translating old texts into modern English. In later life, he translated a fragment of an early version of *The Silmarillion* into Old English. As a device, he implied in his work that *The Hobbit* and *The Lord of the Rings* were modern adaptions of ancient writings. In his fiction, Bilbo Baggins becomes something of a scholar and translates the tales of the Elves into Common Speech; Frodo presents to Sam Gamgee a three volume *Red Book, Translations from the Elvish* by Bilbo.

Some of Tolkien's translations have been published. His rendering of the fourteenth-century Arthurian tale, *Sir Gawain and the Green Knight*, was broadcast by BBC Radio in 1953 and was eventually published in 1975; other translations from the same period include the poem *Pearl*. His retelling of the story of Sigurd and Gudrún from the Old Norse *The Poetic Edda* was published in 2009. This tale of the dragon Fáfnir, and his slaughter by Sigurd, had fired his imagination as a child, retold as it was in Andrew Lang's *Red Fairy Book*. It was to greatly influence Tolkien's

own story of Túrin Turambar and his killing of the dragon named Glaurung in *The Silmarillion*. Tolkien also made a partial translation of the difficult text of *Old English Exodus*.

Intriguingly, Tolkien played a modest part in the first edition of *The Jerusalem Bible* (1966) — an influential English language version of the French *La Bible Jerusalem* — by translating the book of Jonah from the French. There is evidence, however, that he took into account some Hebrew words from the original text of Jonah, in conjunction with a basic lexicon. As agreed Father Anthony Jones, the editor, checked Tolkien's translation against the biblical Hebrew and the ancient Greek translation in the *Septuagent*, and subsequently revised Tolkien's translation.

MASTERY OF THE METRE

*While teaching at Leeds University in the 1920s, Tolkien worked on a verse translation of the great Old English poem, **Beowulf**. He also achieved a complete prose translation, as yet lying unpublished in the Bodleian Library Special Collection, Oxford. His verse translations* *display his remarkable mastery of the metre, a device that was highly developed in Old English, which relied upon alliteration and drew upon the rich resources of natural speech patterns. Furthermore, he made use of this alliterative metre in his unfinished poetic version of a tale from* **The Silmarillion,** *that of Túrin Turambar.*

Invented languages
The foundations of Middle-earth

Integral to J.R.R. Tolkien's world of Middle-earth are his invented languages, which function like real human languages. This is especially evident in the language he developed most: Elvish. Indeed, it was from these invented foundation languages that the peoples, places and the stories of Middle-earth developed.

Elvish was, of course, the language of the Elves, inspired in its chief variants by Tolkien's youthful discovery of both Finnish and Welsh. Tolkien accounts for the formation of these variants – Quenya and Sindarin respectively – by the shaping effect of the history and geography of Middle-earth. The names of beings and places in *The Lord of the Rings* and other stories are often Elvish in origin, which explains their particular character. Elvish can be studied with the aid of Jim Allan's *An Introduction to Elvish* (1978), Ruth S. Noel's *The Languages of Middle-earth* (1980), and glossaries to the volumes of *The History of Middle-earth* (1983–96) as well as other unfinished material by Tolkien that has been edited by his son, Christopher.

Westron, or Common Speech, is the language of mankind and

Egyptian 'Solar barge' of Khufu – Númenorean civilisation in some ways resembled ancient Egypt's

can be traced back to the ancient world. Originally, humans were exposed to Elvish by the Dark Elves who stayed behind when others emigrated far west to Valinor, the land of the angelic powers; in this way, the Dark Elves were to greatly influence the development of the human language. Many human tribes moved to Beleriand, and here Elves and humans intermingled.

At the end of the First Age, Númenor was given to the favoured of mankind; it was there that Westron continued to develop. The Númenoreans were great mariners and colonizers, spreading their civilization, and Westron with it as the language of trade and culture. They also continued to use Elvish as a language of ceremony and tradition, in which the great cosmology and history of the Elves and other peoples was recorded. As Númenor became corrupt, attempts were made to suppress the use of Elvish, but the faithful continued to use it. After the destruction of Númenor, the remaining Númenoreans established the kingdoms of Arnor and Gondor in the north and south of Middle-earth.

Tolkien represents Westron with English in *The Lord of the Rings*, varying his style to match some of its range and diversity; ideally some would have been represented in Old English. For example, the dialect used by the Hobbits is represented quite differently from that of the noble people of Gondor, steeped as they were in the traditions of Elves and Númenor. He retains this device in *The Silmarillion*, where the high Elvish style is represented by deliberate archaisms of syntax and vocabulary. He intends to suggest a contrast in the Elvish source of *The Silmarillion*, and the Hobbitish writing of *The Hobbit* and *The Lord of the Rings*.

The dialect used by the Hobbits has many resemblances to the speech of the men of the River Anduin region, to which the people of Rohan to the south were related, and to Rohirric, the archaic form of Westron used by the people of Rohan. In representing Rohirric in his device of English translation, it was natural for Tolkien to draw upon Old English names and archaic English.

Black Speech was very different

from the languages of Elves, humans and Hobbits. Devised by the evil Sauron in the Second Age of Middle-earth and revived by him in the Third Age, it may have been a perverted form of Elvish. The orcs of Mordor used a crude form of Black Speech, yet the only example of pure Black Speech given in Tolkien's writings is the inscription on the One Ring in *The Lord of the Rings*.

QUENYA AND SINDARIN

The Quenya form of Elvish is used in the undying lands far to the west, and may be close to the original language taught by the Valar, the angelic powers. Quenya shares its ancestry with Sindarin Elvish: both diverge in grammar, vocabulary and sound, but Quenya is less dynamic, being less exposed to geographical and historical influences. Tolkien compares it to the high Latin of church liturgy, and Quenya owes its inspiration to Tolkien's love of Finnish. His use of Quenya in names, quotations, and fragments of song helps to achieve great beauty throughout his stories of Middle-earth. Sindarin was a form of Elvish used by Sindarin or Grey-Elves and owes its inspiration to Tolkien's early love of Welsh, which it structurally resembles. Tolkien accounts for the great changes in Elvish that resulted in Sindarin to the geography and history of Middle-earth. The determining factor is that the Sindarin Elves remained in Beleriand rather than completing the great journey over the sea to the utter West. Sindarin enriched the language of humans, including the later Hobbits, which became Westron.

Something borrowed, something new
Dwarf names in The Hobbit and elsewhere

Most of the dwarves who accompany Bilbo Baggins in *The Hobbit* are called by names borrowed by J.R.R. Tolkien from a list in the ancient Norse *Poetic Edda*, now preserved in Iceland. These borrowed names include Dwalin, Bifur, Bofur, Bombur, Nori, Fíli, Kíli, Dori, Ori, Óin, and Glóin, and their leader Thorin; Gandalf's name is also taken from the same list. The other dwarf in the company is Balin.

In later years Gimli, son of Glóin, accompanies Bilbo's nephew, Frodo Baggins, as one of the Fellowship who support him on his quest to destroy the Ring. After the War of the Ring, he becomes known as Lord of the Glittering Caves as he settles with a group of dwarves he has brought from the north to the caverns of Helm's Deep, known as Aglarond, which is Sindarin Elvish for 'glittering caves, place of glory'. Gimli is also known as Elf-friend because of his devotion to Galadriel and friendship with Legolas the Elf, also of the Fellowship of the Ring.

The dwarves call themselves Khazâd. During the First Age of Middle-earth, Elves call them the Naugrim ('stunted people'); they also call them the Nogothrim or Noegyth. In addition, dwarves are known as Folk of the Mountain. Khazâd-dûm, through which Frodo, Sam and the others of the Fellowship of the Ring pass, means 'dwarf-mansion', yet the Elves usually speak of Khazâd-dûm as Moria, which means 'black-pit'. This place is the greatest of the dwarf-

halls and home to the dwarves before the Balrog hidden deep within the mountains was freed as a result of the deep mining of the precious mithil.

English Place-Names Society
Uncovering a rich history in names of places

Throckmorton, Bag End, Dragon Farm, Dragon School, Dragon Hill, Inkberrow, Morton Underhill, River Shirebourn, Shire Lane, Wood End all are (or were) actual locations in areas of England that J.R.R. Tolkien lived or visited. Sadly Bag End – the ancient name for the farm at which Tolkien's aunt, Jane Neave, worked – no longer exists; it is now a private house named Dormston Manor, but it is still recognizable as the old farm. What is striking is that each of these names might have come from Tolkien's fictional world of Hobbits.

As a professional philologist, all forms of language fascinated the creator of Middle-earth; place names in particular hold a wealth of history. It was because of his fascination for place names that Tolkien became a long-standing member of the English Place-Names Society, which is now based at the University of Nottingham. The scholarly Society began in 1923 with the purpose of carrying out an ambitious survey of place names throughout England.

The Survey's specific aim is to find out how all the country's names began and developed over time. Its publications are arranged by historic counties: the first, which appeared in 1925, featured Buckinghamshire; the eightieth volume, which was published in 2004, concerned just part of Shropshire. At first the Survey limited itself largely to main place names, such as those of villages, towns, forests and larger rivers. However after the Second World War minor names, including field and street names, were also featured owing to their historical and linguistic interest. Newer volumes of the survey are therefore likely to cover smaller areas instead of whole counties at a time.

Taken by storm
J.R.R. Tolkien discovers the Gothic language

Gothic is an old Germanic language that has now become extinct. The Goths were a people first documented to be living in the Black Sea area in the third century AD. Our knowledge of the language derives mainly from the Codex Argenteus, which is a sixth-century copy of the fourth-century translation of the Bible into the Gothic language. Gothic is therefore the only language in the East Germanic group with a substantial body of text still to its name.

The philologist Joseph Wright published a monumental *Grammar of the Gothic Language* in 1910, the full title of this work stretching to *Grammar of the Gothic Language and the Gospel of St Mark, Selections from the Other Gospels and the Second Epistle to Timothy*. As a schoolboy, J.R.R. Tolkien was delighted to acquire a second-hand copy of Wright's earlier title, *Primer of the Gothic Language* (1892). Wright was a Professor at Oxford University and became

The Lord's Prayer written in Gothic

Atta unsar, þu in himinam,

weihnai namo þein,

qimai þiudinassus þeins,

wairþai wilja þeins,

swe in himina jah ana airþai.

Hlaif unsarana þana sinteinan gif
uns himma daga,

jah aflet uns þatei skulans
sijaima,

swaswe jah weis afletam þaim
skulam unsaraim,

jah ni briggais uns in fraistubnjai,

ak lausei uns af þamma ubilin.

Tolkien's lecturer and tutor when
he started studying there in 1910.
During this time, the philologist was
to communicate to Tolkien his love
of languages; he was a demanding
teacher and a formative influence
upon the author's life.

Many years later, describing his
encounter with Gothic, Tolkien wrote
that it was 'a beautiful language'
which reached the 'eminence' of
use in church liturgy. On Wright's
Grammar of the Gothic Language, he
also wrote that he discovered 'for the
first time the study of a language out
of mere love'. Moreover, in a lecture
he confessed that Gothic was the first
language to take him by storm, and to
move his heart.

RECORDING IN GOTHIC

After finishing **The Lord of the
Rings,** *but before its eventual
publication, Tolkien stayed with his
friend George Sayer, the English
Master at Malvern College in
Worcestershire. To entertain his
guest, Sayer pulled out a bulky
open-reel tape recorder. In mock
suspicion of the new-fangled
machine, Tolkien asked, no doubt
with a broad smile, if he could record
the Lord's Prayer in Gothic. When
he heard the recorded result, he was
delighted and requested if he might
record some extracts of* **The Lord
of the Rings;** *the more he recorded,
the more his confidence grew. The
recordings, minus the Gothic, are
available today on audio CD.*

MYTH, MAGIC AND MACHINES

King Arthur casts a spell
Stories of marvels and adventure

Stories of King Arthur cast a spell over J.R.R. Tolkien's childhood, awakening in him a desire for the 'land of Merlin and Arthur' and other worlds, replete with magical creatures such as wizards and fairies, and marvellous yet perilous adventures. As a scholar, he wrote in later years that although Arthur, Guinevere and Lancelot were not fairy beings, 'the good and evil story of Arthur's court is a "fairy story" '.

Tolkien associated the traditional body of King Arthur stories with the Norman Conquest of England in the eleventh century. He preferred to create his own compendium of the legends and myths of Middle-earth; for these he would draw upon stories that predated the conquest and were therefore quintessentially 'English'. Unlike in the writings of his friends C.S. Lewis and Charles Williams, there are few explicitly Arthurian

stories in Tolkien's work. There are, however, some important references to the tales of King Arthur in his stories; these include the departure of Frodo, Gandalf and others for western lands over the sea, which clearly echoes Arthur's passing over to a place of healing in Avalon. Yet, Tolkien transforms any such references to match seamlessly with his own consistent world of Middle-earth.

The main Arthurian tale to be found in Tolkien's work is his translation of and scholarly commentary upon the fourteen-century poem *Sir Gawain and the Green Knight*, a poem he regarded as a masterpiece and clearly wished contemporary readers to share. There is also his long, unfinished poem *The Fall of Arthur*, which has never been published; all we know of this derives from a brief description in the official biography of Tolkien by Humphrey Carpenter. The biographer tells us that Tolkien's poem does not include mention of the Holy Grail, recounting the tale of King Arthur taking part in war abroad in 'Saxon lands' accompanied by his knight Sir Gawain; when Arthur receives

The original manuscript of Sir Gawain *and the Green Knight*

news of the treachery of Mordred, he returns home. In Tolkien's unusual portrayal Queen Guinevere is ruthless and intent on evil, although as beautiful as a fairy woman; indeed, Mordred is gripped by a powerful sexual obsession for her.

Númenor
Tolkien's island of Atlantis

The lost island of Atlantis is a familiar element of Western myth and legend; it has held a constant appeal to the human imagination for thousands of years. The clearest and most influential account of it is to be found in the writings of the ancient Greek philosopher, Plato. So it is intriguing to learn that, beginning in childhood, Tolkien had a recurring dream of a great flood, led by a great, surging green wave. Eventually, after a long gestation, this dream became part of his imagined world of Middle-earth as he told of the destruction of Númenor, his mythological counterpart to the ancient Atlantis.

In Tolkien's myth, Númenor is a star-shaped island kingdom given to the Elf-friends of mankind who had resisted Morgoth, the first Dark Lord, at the close of the First Age of Middle-earth. Far over the western seas, Númenor is situated between the enormous landmass of Middle-earth to its east and the undying lands of the Valar to its west.

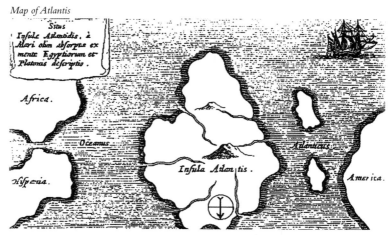

Map of Atlantis

Although barely distinguishable from Elves in their nobility, the Númenoreans are mortal like humans, but live to a far greater age.

The fall of Númenor

The fall of the Númenoreans is divine punishment for disobeying the prohibition to set foot in the distant immortal lands. A malicious figure that plays a part in the downfall of the island kingdom is Sauron, at that time attractive in appearance and seductive of speech. After the fall, the entire world of Middle-earth is turned into a sphere and the seas are bent. It becomes impossible for humans to find a path to the undying lands; the only way lies in a lost road.

A section of *The Silmarillion*, published after Tolkien's death in 1977, forms an account of the downfall of Númenor; it is entitled the 'Akallabêth' meaning 'the downfallen'. In addition, an incomplete work published in *Sauron Defeated* provides readers with a fascinating take on Númenor and its downfall: *The Notion Club Papers* is a science-fiction story involving a form of time travel, its purpose being to introduce to readers the tales of the lost island far off in the western sea. The time travelling links modern Oxford with the ancient island civilisation, the effects of whose destruction intrudes into the present world as a great storm.

NOBLE REMNANT

Númenor's fate plays an important role in the history of Middle-earth, because a faithful remnant of the noble race who flee its destruction found the great kingdoms of Arnor in the north and Gondor in the south. Eventually Aragorn, one of the descendants of the kings disguised as a Ranger, becomes a companion of Frodo Baggins in his quest to destroy the Great Ring of Sauron.

The 'Ainulindalë'
Creation of the world by music

At the centre of J.R.R. Tolkien's mythology of Middle-earth is his account of the creation of the world. Although a God-like figure is not mentioned directly in *The Lord of the Rings*, Tolkien's portrayal of the earlier Ages in

The Silmarillion begins with the 'Ainulindalë' in which Ilúvatar, or 'father of all', is introduced as the divine creator of all things. Tolkien's account of the creation of the world by Ilúvatar is one of his finest pieces of writing, which turns theology and philosophy into literary art.

The 'Ainulindalë' introduces events before the creation of the physical world but not before the creation of the angelic powers who will assist Ilúvatar in shaping the world. These angelic powers or 'gods' are known as the Ainur. The 'Ainulindalë' or 'song of the Ainur' recounts how, prior to the ages of Middle-earth, Ilúvatar created the world. First he presents his idea of it in music to the listening powers. Then he brings what is musically foreshadowed into physical being with the help of his angelic agents. *The Silmarillion* goes on to chronicle the history of the Elves and their interactions with mankind.

Ilúvatar's music forms blueprints or patterns of the world that is to be, and expresses his care for what he is to create. Tolkien calls these prefigurations that will determine the world the 'themes' of the divine

Kepler's The Music of the Spheres: Tolkien drew upon a common ancient belief of music behind the universe

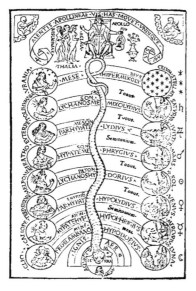

development of the world is revealed; the divine music overcomes the discord, taking up Melkor's jarring notes to enhance the sound. In the third theme, the angelic powers play no part. This theme has as its subject the creation by God himself of 'The Children of Ilúvatar'; that is, Elves and humans. In this way, the music of the Ainur concerns the 'growth and flowering' of divine thought as the world is first created, and then develops in the histories of Elves and humankind.

music. The holy music develops three themes of Ilúvatar the Creator. The first theme, in which the angelic powers are allowed to participate in the music, presents the initial formation of the yet-to-be-created world. Into this theme the renegade Morgoth (then called Melkor) introduces discord as a result of his rebellion. In the second theme the

INSPIRATION FOR NARNIA?

The 'Ainulindalë' may well have inspired C.S. Lewis when he portrayed the creation of Narnia by the song of Aslan, the Creator-Lion, in **The Magician's Nephew** *(1955). Although it was written before* **The Silmarillion** *and the* **The Lord of the Rings** *were published, Lewis had already heard his friend Tolkien read the 'Ainulindalë' so was well aware of its contents.*

Mythopoeia
J.R.R. Tolkien's manifesto in verse

'Mythopoeia' literally means 'the making of myth', and is also the name of a poem written in rhyming couplets that J.R.R. Tolkien wrote and addressed to his friend, C.S. Lewis. At that time Lewis, who for many years had been an atheist, held sceptical views about the role of imagination in shaping our knowledge and had spoken of poetry representing 'lies breathed through silver', but lies nevertheless. As a devout Christian, Tolkien was trying to persuade Lewis of a wider view of reality by defending the role of the imagination, and well as that of stories and myth, in achieving truth.

His poem *Mythopoeia* is written from Philomythus to Misomythus – that is, from a lover to a distruster of myth. In this, Tolkien actually recorded the essences of a long conversation held at night on Addison's Walk in Oxford's Magdalen College in 1931, as well as many previous exchanges with Lewis. That conversation was to have a deep impact upon C.S. Lewis, as it was the final event that resulted in him moving from atheism to Christian belief, the end of a long process.

Tolkien's poem *Mythopoeia* provides a good idea of the flow of the conversation. On the basis of our universal love of story and myth, he argued in favour of the validity of the Christian Gospels. He wrote of the human heart not being composed of falsehood; rather, it receives nourishment of knowledge from the Wise One and remembers him still. Although the estrangement is ancient, human beings are neither completely abandoned by God nor totally corrupted; although disgraced, we still retain the tatters of our mandate to rule. We continue to create according to the 'law in which we're made'. In this poem, Tolkien reveals his basic

Addison's Walk at Magdalen College, Oxford

beliefs, his way of seeing the world, and the ideas behind his fiction.

Harmony of story and fact

C.S. Lewis later wrote a powerful essay, which adds further understanding to the meaning of Tolkien's poem *Mythopoeia*. In it, Lewis describes the harmony of story and fact in the Christian Gospels. They have all the elements that appeal to the human imagination, which we find in poetry and stories, while at the same time being embedded in actual human history and real individual events. As C.S. Lewis puts it: 'This is the marriage of heaven and earth, perfect Myth and Perfect Fact: claiming not only our love and Obedience, but also our wonder and delight, addressed to the savage, the child, and the poet in each one of us no less than to the moralist, the scholar, and the philosopher.'

The grave of J.R.R. and Edith Tolkien at Wolvercote cemetery, Oxford

Beren and Lúthien
A very personal myth

The story of the love between Aragorn and Arwen is an important thread in *The Lord of the Rings*; it echoes an ancient tale of the lovers Beren and Lúthien from the First Age of Middle-earth. In his journey with them from Bree to Rivendell, Aragorn, then known to his Hobbit companions as Strider, briefly retells the story of Beren and Lúthien to Frodo, Sam and the others beside Weathertop; the story is told more fully in *The Silmarillion*.

In the story Lúthien, Elven daughter of King Thingol and Queen Melian of the wooded realm of Doriath, has great powers and

beauty. To win her as his wife, Beren cuts a Silmaril – a precious gem containing original light of the world – from the Iron Crown of Morgoth, the principal angelic power who turned to evil. After being slayed by Carcharoth, Morgoth's huge wolf, Beren is allowed to return to life after Lúthien's intercession in the houses of the dead, and after her choice of a life of human span instead of immortality. The two then live happily in Ossiriand, to the east of Beleriand, an area of Middle-earth that existed at that time but would be engulfed by sea in later Ages.

Lúthien's sacrificial love for Beren leads to the most significant union of an Elf with a human being and clearly illustrates J.R.R. Tolkien's persistent theme of immortality and death. Tolkien regarded the story of Beren and Lúthien as the pivotal one of *The Silmarillion*, and the key to its interlocking themes and events. The tale also determines the outcome of events for Ages to come, not least in its intermarriage of an Elven princess and a mortal man, by which the deeply spiritual quality of the Elves becomes incarnate in humanity.

J.R.R. TOLKIEN'S GRAVE

J.R.R. Tolkien and his wife, Edith, are buried together in Wolvercote cemetery, north Oxford, where the headstone adds the names 'Beren' and 'Lúthien' to the grave's identifying inscription. Tolkien associated his love for Edith with the story of Beren and Lúthien, owing in part to an incident that occurred early in their married life when he was convalescing from the trauma of fighting in the Battle of the Somme. In a woodland clearing close to Roos in Yorkshire, Edith had danced for him; in the story, Beren first encounters Lúthien dancing at moonrise in a forest. Beren calls her Tinúviel, which means 'nightingale', or 'daughter of twilight', in Elvish.

The Ring that rules
Sauron's ultimate machine

The Great, Ruling, or One Ring is treacherously made by Sauron to control the other Rings of the Elves, the dwarves and mankind; the story of this Ring shapes the events

told in *The Lord of the Rings*. At the end of the Second Age of Middle-earth, after the original downfall of Sauron who eventually becomes the Dark Lord, King Isildur takes possession of the Ring, but loses it in the River Anduin. There it lies for centuries until possessed, after murder, by Gollum. As *The Hobbit* tells us, he is to bear it for centuries until Bilbo Baggins stumbles upon him in caverns deep within the Misty Mountains. *The Lord of the Rings* records how Bilbo reluctantly dispossesses himself of the Ring, passing it to his nephew, Frodo Baggins. Frodo takes on the task of destroying the Ring in the very heart of Mordor, which is the only way its power of evil can be stopped forever.

Gandalf interprets the significance of the Ring vividly at the last debate in Gondor. The wizard warns the leaders of the triumphant armies of the West that they have not won the final victory over Sauron; this cannot be accomplished by military might. He tells them that their only hope of victory lies in the destruction of the Ring. If Sauron regains it, his victory will be so total that his power may last until the end of the world; however, if the Ring is destroyed his fall will be so complete that he may never rise again. Sauron has invested most of his power in the Ring and is thus intrinsically linked to its fate; through its destruction the world will be rid of a great evil.

The ultimate machine

Sauron is a supreme technocrat and the Ring is a product of his technological skill, in which he imbues part of himself; the Ring is the ultimate machine. In his writings, J.R.R. Tolkien makes a clear distinction between art and this kind of dark magic. Art is typified in the Elves, who have no desire to dominate others in the way Sauron does. Tolkien saw the story of the Ring as having resonance in today's world: he felt that machines have the potential to be the modern form of dark magic, which seeks to control and possess human beings and the natural world.

Some of Tolkien's rather similar reflections on the subject are to be found scattered throughout his correspondence. For instance, he reveals his understanding that Sauron's Ring is essentially a machine made to objectify his power and in a letter to his son, Christopher, he describes the Second World as 'the first War of the Machines'. Tolkien's friend C.S. Lewis thought and imagined along similar lines. In a lecture some years after the Seconf World War, Lewis labelled his times as the 'Age of the Machine'; we are in an epoch, he argued, as significant as a Stone Age or an Iron Age.

THE ATOMIC BOMB?
*When **The Lord of the Rings** first appeared, some interpreted the One Ring to represent the atomic bomb. Apart from the fact that the Ring was part of his story before the bomb was even invented, Tolkien felt that such interpretations imposed a very limited meaning upon his creation. Indeed, he believed that the story could be interpreted in many ways according to the 'thought and experience of readers', some of these ways not even anticipated by its author. Forced interpretations, like that of equating the Ring with the atomic bomb, wrongly assumed that he was attempting to dominate his readers.*

British at heart
J.R.R. Tolkien and Celtic mythology

J.R.R. Tolkien insisted, rather emphatically, that his stories of Middle-earth were not Celtic. Unlike Wales, Scotland and Ireland, England did not have a consistent mythology that could be called English and it became clear that he was trying to create a body of legends, myths and other material that would belong to England alone.

However, his creation of Middle-earth does contain many Celtic elements, and this can be seen in both

Saint Brendan of Clonfert

its development and in its mature forms. Tolkien's own library of books contained many studies of Celtic matters, including medieval myth and folklore, as well as languages. His stories contain plots and patterns of imagery from Celtic sources. Furthermore Welsh, a Celtic language, provided the inspiration for one of the two main branches of his invented Elvish, namely Sindarin. In a lecture entitled 'English and Welsh' given at Oxford the day after the publication of *The Return of the King*, Tolkien spoke of the attraction that the Welsh language held for him. He also told of the growth of his love of language, in which Welsh had played an important part. He is, he says, 'British at heart'.

In an interview with Colin Duriez, literary scholar Dimitra Fimi spoke of Celtic influences in the shaping of Tolkien's mythology of Middle-earth: 'In *The Book of Lost Tales* (the earliest version of what later became *The Silmarillion*), the Irish legend of the Tuatha Dé Danann already played an important role as an inspiration for the tragic story of the Gnomes's (later the Noldor Elves) departure from Valinor…The idea of Valinor itself, of an Otherworld in the West, is also associated with Celtic material, particularly the Irish legend of St Brendan (which Tolkien used also…) The story of Beren and Lúthien, one of the "great tales" of the mythology, uses a strong Celtic motif: the love of a fairy woman and a mortal man, and it has been often compared with the tale of "Culwch and Olwen" from the Welsh *Mabinogion*.'

Tolkien's poem about St Brendan is called simply *Imram*, which is Gaelic for 'voyage'. In this, he transposed the story of St Brendan's famous early medieval voyage into his invented mythology. His poem mentions a 'shoreless mountain' (Meneltarma) marking 'the foundered land' (Númenor), a mysterious island (Tol Eressëa) with a white Tree (Celeborn), and a beautiful star (Eärendil) marking the old road leading beyond the world.

Furthermore, Tolkien's narrative poem *The Lay of Aotrou and Itroun* uses Celtic folklore. The title means 'Lord and Lady', and the poem was inspired by the Celtic legends of Brittany, a land that shares close linguistic links with Wales. A childless Lord obtains a potion from a Corrigan, a fairy enchantress, which results in the birth of twins. When the Corrigan demands that the Lord marries her as payment, he refuses on Christian principle, accepting that he will die as a consequence.

Northern mythology
A desire for an older world

An important source of J.R.R. Tolkien's inspiration – apart from the biblical roots of his orthodox Christianity – was the languages and literature of northern Europe. This is to give a non-technical label to the wide influences of Germanic languages and literature, including Old Norse, as well as the non-Germanic language and literature of Finland. Tolkien thought that a language as much as its literature carried in it a sometimes hidden mythology, body of legends, worldview or belief system. Particular works of literature that were an

Mímir and Baldr consulting the Norns (in northern myth, Norns are female fates controlling the destines of both gods and humans)

important source or influence upon Tolkien include: the *Elder* or *Poetic Edda*, the later *Prose Edda*, the *Saga of the Völsungs*, *The Kalevala*, *Beowulf*, and *The Battle of Maldon*. Additionally, Old Norse and Old English heavily influenced Middle-English literature, and works from this period such as *Sir Gawain and the Green Knight* also influenced Tolkien's work.

Tolkien shared with C.S. Lewis a love of 'northernness': a quality in stories, art and music that Lewis described in his autobiography, *Surprised by Joy* (1955). Lewis relates that he discovered this quality when he came across the death of the god Balder in a poem by Longfellow: 'I knew nothing about Balder; but instantly I was uplifted into huge regions of northern sky. I desired with almost sickening intensity something never to be described (except that it is cold, spacious, severe, pale and remote) and then...found myself at the very same moment already falling out of that desire and wishing I were back in it.'

Time travel
A desire to experience the past

Sometime before J.R.R. Tolkien began writing *The Lord of the Rings*, his friend C.S. Lewis remarked to him that there was too little around of what they both enjoyed in modern stories. They therefore decided that one of them should write on space, and the other on time; they tossed a coin and the result was that Tolkien got time travel. He made two attempts to write stories of time travel – one being *The Lost Road* and the other, *The Notion Club Papers* – yet completed neither. Each was designed as a route for readers into the compendium of tales, mythology and other material of *The Silmarillion*.

Both his unfinished attempts are different from his main body of fiction in that they feature twentieth-century characters and settings. Furthermore, neither has a gadget like a time machine; instead, time travel occurs through memories and persistent dreams, and by following clues in unusual words of a forgotten language. From his other writings, we can see that these are words

J.R.R. TOLKIEN'S INVENTED WORLD

Middle-earth
The world that Tolkien invented

Tolkien discovered as he invented the languages that undergird his tales and material concerning Middle-earth.

The dreams of the characters evoke memories inherited from sometimes very distant ancestors, the end result being that they eventually directly experience the past that Tolkien describes in his world of Middle-earth. In both unfinished stories, the Middle-earth events experienced by the time travellers are set in or concern Númenor, the island civilisation ultimately destroyed by a catastrophe in which the very shape of the world is changed.

Middle-earth is the name that identifies J.R.R. Tolkien's invented world of *The Hobbit*, *The Lord of the Rings*, and a mass of writing left unfinished by Tolkien at his death, later published as *The Silmarillion*, *Unfinished Tales* and other books. Middle-earth can refer to the whole world, or just to the landmass east of the great sea of Belegaer.

The cosmos Tolkien envisaged is complex and developed over the long years he spent creating Middle-earth. The blessed realm of Valinor, home of the angelic powers, was originally on a vast continent west of the great sea, where it could then be reached by sea from the east, travelling from Beleriand and other regions. This became increasingly difficult, because of the disobedience of the Noldor, the group of Elves swayed by the rebellious leader, Fëanor.

The events of the First Age

Map of northwest Europe

of Middle-earth are set on a flat world. In the Second Age, after the destruction of the island civilisation of Númenor, the shape of the world changes and it becomes the sphere we know. The undying region of Valinor is removed from the physical geography of the world, although it was still a real place.

Middle-earth is the setting of the planned habitation of mankind. Although Elves originate here, they are called on the great journey to the utter west to be with the Valar; the Elves who stay in Middle-earth, or return to it from Valinor, enrich the life and language of humans. Eventually, most Elves pass from Middle-earth but leave their mark genetically on mankind, epitomized in the marriage of the elf-maiden Lúthien to the mortal Beren.

THE REAL MIDDLE-EARTH

Tolkien did not invent the name 'Middle-earth'; it is simply a modern form of an ancient name for the home of mankind. It occurs, for instance, as the Anglo-Saxon 'middungeard' in the very early 'Hymn to God' of Caedmon of Whitby. Tolkien intended the setting of his stories to be our real world but in an imaginary time, forming a kind of alternative history. The 'real' Middle-earth is therefore intended to be the world we know, but imagined many thousands of years ago, before Christ. Tolkien specifically intended that its landscapes and geographical features would evoke a sense of familiarity, especially for readers in northwest Europe.

A cosmic battle
*Angels and demons in
J.R.R. Tolkien's stories*

In J.R.R. Tolkien's mythology, the angelic powers called the Valar first existed in a time before the creation of Middle-earth and the cosmos in which it lay. Tolkien portrays the Valar as being like the gods of the pagan world of northern and classical mythology. However, he takes the Valar further by casting them as angelic beings;

Gustav Doré's Satan

they only take the place of the gods of mythology in an imaginative sense. In theological terms, they are merely angels – messengers and agents of Ilúvatar (God).

Theologically, the Valar are the creations of Ilúvatar, the father of all, and are made to serve him; they are not beings to be worshipped. Although in this Tolkien is seeking to be true to his Christian worldview, interestingly he extends the role of the Valar to assist Ilúvatar in the creation of the world. Moreover, Ilúvatar allows them freedom and creativity in how they accomplish what is in his mind; he discloses his vision for creation to the Valar in music, to provide them with a splendid blueprint.

There is conflict in heaven as Melkor (Morgoth) rebels, taking with him many lesser angelic powers called Maiar. This rebellion enters Ilúvatar's music of creation as discord, which is resolved by the divine composer into a new harmony, revealing that evil in the world will not last forever. The fall of Melkor effectively retells the story of Satan and the angels who fell, thus becoming demons. The grand actions of Tolkien's heavenly beings and their complex role in the events of Middle-earth lend a larger perspective to the struggles between good and evil in the lives of the Elves, humans, Hobbits and other races featured in Tolkien's stories.

SAURON, TOLKIEN'S REPLACEMENT DEVIL

Sauron, the Dark Lord of **The Lord of the Rings**, *was one of the lesser angelic powers called Maiar, and in earlier years was the principal lieutenant of the great Melkor, later Morgoth. This was before Melkor was finally banished and thrown into the Void, at which point Sauron took his place as the leading protagonist of evil, or Tolkien's Satan figure. Sauron's technological skills assisted in the creation of the Rings of Power by the Elves of Eregion. His devilry was most evident in deceitfully forging the One Ring to rule all the others: the ring was a supreme machine with a form of powerful artificial intelligence into which he placed most of his powers.*

From Elves to humans
The history of Elves and humans in Middle-earth

Middle-earth is strictly only part of the world. Before the cataclysmic change in the geography of the world after the destruction of Númenor, the Undying Lands of the West including Valinor are physically part of this world. Indeed, the history of Elves, as told in *The Silmarillion*, incorporates events in Valinor and its impact upon humans.

J.R.R. Tolkien wanted to make a consistent world, and this is why much of his invention concerned the history, as well as annals, languages, chronology, and geography of Middle-earth. There are a number of major tales that are intended to stand independently of the history of Middle-earth, recorded in *The Silmarillion*. That history is an imaginatively appealing backdrop to such tales as those of Beren and Lúthien the elf-maiden, Túrin Turambar, Tuor and the Fall of Gondolin, the Voyage of Eärendil the Mariner, *The Hobbit* and *The Lord of the Rings*.

The Sindarin word 'gwilwileth' meaning 'butterfly'

As a prologue to the history of Middle-earth, Tolkien also invents a beautiful myth of origins, *The Ainulindalë*, portraying events before the creation of the world, which determine its shape and development. The history is dominated by the themes of death and decline, as the immortal Elves live out a long defeat before they fade from the world, leaving mankind in ascendance and spiritually enriched.

The Ages of Middle-earth
The rise and decline of the Elves

There are several Ages of Middle-earth. Prior to these, Ilúvatar creates the world, first in thought expressed in the music of creation, and then by giving the world actual being. Before the beginning of the First Age, marked by the rising of the sun, the Valar and later also many of the Elves are established in the uttermost West, or Valinor.

In the First Age, one of the greatest of the Elves named Fëanor makes the magnificent gems known as light-bearing Silmarils, which provide the underlying motif for *The Silmarillion*. Melkor or Morgoth, a renegade angelic power, darkens Middle-earth by destroying the Two Lamps, and brings shadow to Valinor by extinguishing the Two Trees; he subsequently hides in the cold regions of Middle-earth, north of Beleriand. In the First Age, the northwest region of Beleriand is the setting for the tales of Beren and Lúthien the Elf-maiden, Túrin Turambar, and the Fall of Gondolin. During this Age, Eärendil the Mariner sets sail to Valinor to intercede on behalf of the troubled peoples of Beleriand and eventually Morgoth is cast out of the world.

The later Ages

In the Second Age, the star-shaped island of Númenor is given to the Men of the West who have been faithful in resisting Morgoth. Sauron, Melkor's lieutenant, secretly forges the great Ring in Middle-earth. He succeeds in aiding the corruption of Númenor, resulting in its destruction. After this, the world is changed into a globe, leaving Valinor no longer accessible, except via the Straight Road. There is a great and successful Western alliance against Sauron's forces on behalf of Morgoth. In the Third Age, the Ring remains lost for many centuries; Gondor becomes a great power; and the Hobbits migrate over the Misty Mountains to The Shire. Much later in this Age, the events of *The Hobbit* and *The Lord of the Rings* take place.

The Fourth Age and beyond represents our present era of mankind's domination and the fading of the Elves, where the Christian era unfolds. The original geography of Middle-earth becomes known in its present shape although some parts, such as early twentieth-century Warwickshire and Worcestershire,

resemble part of that original world, The Shire, quite remarkably. In Tolkien's unfinished stories, an Anglo-Saxon called Aelfwine voyages to the island of Tol Eressëa and, in our own time, Alboin and his son Audoin find the lost road via ancestral dreams, travelling back in time to Númenor.

The Book of Lost Tales
The first version of Middle-earth stories

The Book of Lost Tales comprises the first two volumes of *The History of Middle-earth*, a series of 12 volumes of J.R.R. Tolkien's unfinished or preliminary material, edited and published after his death by his son, Christopher, who also provides a detailed commentary. The other volumes in the series are: *The Lays of Beleriand; The Shaping of Middle-earth; The Lost Road and Other Writings*; the four titles that comprise *The History of The Lord of the Rings; Morgoth's Ring; The War of the Jewels;* and *The Peoples of Middle-earth.*

The Book of Lost Tales represents Tolkien's first major imaginative work. He began it during the First World

War, after seeing action in the Battle of the Somme and being sent back to England to convalesce; he abandoned writing it several years afterwards. The first volume contains narratives relating to Valinor, the Undying Lands to the uttermost West of Middle-earth; the second comprises stories set in Beleriand, during the First Age.

Tolkien attempted to put his stories and poems, which developed in a fervent burst of creativity, into an accessible framework. Thus, *The Book of Lost Tales* describes the story of Aelfwine who, by chance, sails to Tol Eressëa, an Elven island close by the coast of Valinor. There he discovers The Cottage of Lost Play, where he is told the tales of the creation of the world, Morgoth's destruction of the light of the Two Trees of Valinor, and other stories. There are significant differences in detail between this and the final form of the stories presented in *The Silmarillion* but they are clearly recognizable. In *The Book of Lost Tales*, one finds the only full narratives of the Necklace of the Dwarves and the Fall of Gondolin.

Visualizing Middle-earth
The illustrators of Tolkien's world

It is fascinating to learn that J.R.R. Tolkien developed great skills as an illustrator; his visualization of settings from his fiction is of particular interest. Those from *The Silmarillion*, such as illustrations of the Elven realm of Nargothrond, are especially valuable, as the book remained unfinished. The stories of that period – the earlier Ages of Middle-earth – are not filled out as vividly as those in *The Hobbit* and *The Lord of the Rings*, yet Tolkien's illustrations emphasize the great care he always took in visualizing and creating his landscapes and geography of Middle-earth. In his pictures, we glimpse Tol Sirion with the shadow of Thangorodrim on the horizon; we see the beautiful city of Gondolin encircled by mountains; and there is a powerful depiction of Taniquetil, its peak amongst the stars.

Two years after the publication of *The Silmarillion*, and six years after his death, the book *Pictures by J.R.R. Tolkien* (1979) appeared, compiled by his son, Christopher.

This large format title contains 48 sections of paintings, drawings and designs, mostly relating to *The Hobbit*, *The Lord of the Rings* and *The Silmarillion*. From the Third Age of Middle-earth is included Tolkien's crayon drawing of the Mallorn trees of Lórien in Spring, capturing the spiritual quality of the region. There are many other illustrations, including a picture of Hobbiton that was the frontispiece to the original edition of *The Hobbit* in 1937. Here, one of Tolkien's illustrations of Mirkwood is based on an earlier painting of Taur-nu-Fuin, illustrating Beleg's finding of Gwindor. The depiction of the Elvenking's Gate from *The Hobbit* is somewhat reminiscent of Tolkien's earlier portrayal of Nargothrond. One of Tolkien's beautiful, stylized drawings of trees, reproduced in this book, is used on the cover of *Tree and Leaf*; a more naturalistic crayon drawing powerfully depicts Old Man Willow.

Since then, the publication of two other significant books has increased access to Tolkien's illustrations. One is *Tolkien: Life and Legend* (1992), edited by Judith Priestman. The Bodleian Library, Oxford, published

this in conjunction with a major exhibition of Tolkien's manuscripts, maps and illustrations, as well as photographs of biographical interest, held to celebrate the centenary of Tolkien's birth. The other provides a thorough and perceptive exploration of Tolkien's art throughout his life, and includes a large number of quality reproductions. This is *J.R.R. Tolkien: Artist and Illustrator* (1995), by Wayne C. Hammond and Christina Scull. The authors explain that their 'purpose in this book is to show, as widely as possible, the unsuspected range of Tolkien's art, and to relate it both to his life and to the writings for which he is most renowned'.

As well as publishing his own illustrations in *The Hobbit*, Tolkien illustrated other stories for children, which were not published until after his death. One was *Roverandom*, which was inspired by a family holiday in Filey, on the Yorkshire coast. Tolkien's young son, Michael, lost his little dog on the beach. In sympathy, his father told and later wrote down the story about a real dog, Rover, turned into a toy by a wizard. Another story also belonged to this period of Tolkien's life when his children were young. Like the story of the dog Rover, *Mr Bliss* is illustrated in colour throughout by its author. The character, Mr Bliss, is noted for his tall hats, lives in a tall house, and buys a bright yellow car for five shillings. *The Father Christmas Letters* (1976) was not prepared as a book by Tolkien; it is a collection of letters to his children in the 1920s and 1930s, which he writes annually as from Father Christmas, illustrating them vividly.

Other illustrators

Many other talented illustrators have visualized Tolkien's imagination, particularly since the 1960s, when his stories started to become a global phenomenon. Their work has been disseminated in books, calendars, prints and other formats. To name just some, they include Pauline Baynes, John Howe, Alan Lee, Ted Nasmith, Cor Blok, Michael Hague, Rodney Matthews, Roger Garland, and Ruth Lacon. John Howe and Alan Lee are also conceptual artists and illustrators for Peter Jackson's cinematic portrayals of *The Lord of the Rings* and *The Hobbit*.

PAULINE BAYNES

J.R.R. Tolkien chose Pauline Baynes as his preferred illustrator when he spotted some of her artwork at his publishers, which she sent in as unsolicited submissions while seeking work as an unknown artist. Pauline Baynes was to illustrate a range of Tolkien's fiction and poetry: **Farmer Giles of Ham, The Adventures of Tom Bombadil, Smith of Wootton Major, 'Leaf by Niggle',** *and* **'The Homecoming of Beorhtnoth Beorhthelm's Son'.** *Her association with Tolkien's works also became familiar through poster maps and*

Pauline Baynes

cover artwork, famously for the first one-volume paperback edition of **The Lord of the Rings** *(1968).*

Music in Middle-earth
The magical power behind creation

Music and song are a vital thread that runs through J.R.R. Tolkien's tales of Middle-earth. This thread is first introduced with the creation music of Ilúvatar, father of all. Before the creation of the world, its character and development is expressed in music; the presence of evil is prefigured in a discord introduced to this creation music by Morgoth (Melkor), a discord that Ilúvatar is able to harness into a greater ultimate harmony.

The Hobbit and *The Lord of the Rings* include songs that are integral to the story. In addition, Tolkien wrote major sections of his developing mythology in verse, which although not song is closer to music than prose. Modern composers such as Donald Swann, Stephen Oliver and Howard Shore have been able to set songs from Middle-earth to music with great effect. A love of song is characteristic of Elves and Hobbits; furthermore, the character Tom Bombadil's very speech is song or poetry.

Song is also part of the narrative action in key stories of the First Age. For example, in the tale of Beren and Lúthien the Elf-maiden, the Elven-king Finrod Felagund battles with Sauron in song; Lúthien's singing destroys Sauron's tower at Tol Sirion; and in Doriath, her singing enchants Beren, as her mother's singing had enchanted her father Thingol in earlier days. In the tale of Túrin Turambar, after Túrin finds healing at the Pools of Ivrin, he is able to make a song for his lost friend Beleg and is thus able to act once more in defiance of the enemy.

In the Third Age, this power of song seems only to be experienced by Galadriel, one of the greatest of the Elves. Her lament sung in Lórien, while the Company of the Ring were present, makes mention of this power. However, it seems simply a memory of this power, for in that song she only remembers singing of golden leaves, after which golden leaves had appeared; similarly, she only remembered singing of wind, after which a wind blew through the branches.

THE ROAD GOES EVER ON: A SONG CYCLE

In his book **The Road Goes Ever On: A Song Cycle** *(1968, 1978), Donald Swann sets poems by Tolkien written on the theme of the road to music. Musical scores are included, along with notes upon and translations of Elvish poems by J.R.R. Tolkien. The first edition included: 'The Road Goes Ever On'; 'Upon the Hearth the Fire is Red'; 'In the Willow-Meads of Tasarinan'; 'In Western Lands'; 'Namarie (Farewell)'; 'I Sit Beside the Fire'; and 'Errantry'. In the second edition, 'Bilbo's Last Song' was added. A recording of the poems was made, entitled* **Poems and Songs of Middle-earth**, *and sung by William Elvin; the composer himself played the piano.*

Fish and chips
A grasp on the familiar

In *The Lord of the Rings*, the Hobbit Sam Gamgee says to Gollum: 'If you turn over a new leaf, and keep it turned, I'll cook you some taters one of these days. I will; fried fish and chips served by S. Gamgee.' J.R.R. Tolkien suggests that his stories are set in our familiar world several thousand years before Christ; yet if this is indeed the case, why does Sam mention fish and chips?

In fact, this is just one example of Tolkien's creative use of anachronism in his work. That is, he deliberately references places, things and customs, or uses turns of speech, that do not belong to the time and place of his story. What is interesting is that most go unnoticed by readers, carried along as they are by the power of his storytelling. Nevertheless, a careful

reading will uncover many such anachronisms, such as pipe-smoking, English pubs like The Ivy Bush, and references to railway trains and a daily postal service. One important anachronism is The Shire of the Hobbits itself, which is modelled upon the rural Warwickshire and Worcestershire that Tolkien knew as a child, and upon one hamlet in particular named Sarehole near Sarehole Mill, then in the countryside close to Birmingham.

An explanation that Tolkien provides, which carefully does not draw the reader's attention from the 'believability' of his story, is that *The Hobbit* and *The Lord of the Rings* have been translated into English from an older text. The story, Tolkien pretends, was originally written in Common Speech or Westron, a language in general use by Hobbits and other races of Middle-earth. The translation into English, by implication, draws upon many of today's equivalents. Tolkien's real purpose is to give his reader a sense of familiarity on which to grasp when taken into the stranger realms of the story, especially once The Shire is left behind.

Tom Shippey, a writer on Tolkien, puts it like this when speaking of the story *The Hobbit*: 'It takes its readers, even child readers, into a totally unfamiliar world, but then indicates to them that it is not totally unfamiliar, that they have a birth-right in it of their own.' Certainly, when Sam Gamgee presents the amusing situation of offering the temperamental Gollum fish and chips – to whom the idea of 'scorching' fish is outrageous – he along with Frodo Baggins are about to face the perils of entering the Dark Lord Sauron's stronghold of Mordor. This clashing contrast helps us to retain a grasp on the familiar and ordinary as we encounter the horrors of Shelob, then the hellish world of orc-ridden Mordor.

IMAGINED CHARACTERS AND MAGICAL CREATURES

Aragorn
The epic hero figure

In *The Lord of the Rings*, Aragorn is a leading member of the Company of the Ring that accompanies Frodo Baggins as he sets out on his quest to destroy the One Ring. In disguise as a Ranger of the north, protecting The Shire of the Hobbits, Frodo and the other Hobbits first encounter Aragorn at the inn at Bree as a cloaked and hooded figure known as Strider. At first unknown to his companions, he is in fact the true heir to the ancient human king, Isildur; after the War of the Ring he is crowned, and restores the old northern and southern kingdoms.

Aragon is the main epic hero in *The Lord of the Rings*, representing the ideal king of the old West and combining many heroic qualities. He is a healer, a guardian and wise man, as well as warrior whose command even the dead acknowledge. In fact, he is the Beren of his Age: Beren, in a distant Age of Middle-earth, married an Elf of great beauty called Lúthien; Arwen, Aragorn's great love, resembles Lúthien in beauty and virtue, and like her renounces immortality in marrying a human. Aragorn retells the story of Beren and Lúthien to Frodo, Sam and the others beside Weathertop, as they travel from The Shire at the start of Frodo's quest.

Moreover, Aragorn is a true king, whose return is heralded in ancient prophecy. Indeed, J.R.R. Tolkien provides him with the characteristics of an ideal king: his healing hands and humility, his sacrifice of years as a Ranger, and his power over evil. Tolkien was inspired in his depiction of Aragorn by his rich knowledge of the medieval world with its ideals of good kingship, particularly in the teachings of the philosopher, St Thomas Aquinas. In Aragorn, the wisdom of the destroyed island of Númenor is restored.

Frodo and the Company of the Ring find Aragorn a wise companion, and a strong leader after the loss of Gandalf in Khazad-dûm, in the darkness of Moria. Aragorn's strategy of passing through the Paths of the Dead helps to bring victory in the War of the Ring; and after fighting in that dreadful battle, Éowyn, the White Lady of Rohan, and her companion-in-arms, Merry the Hobbit, find healing at his hands. In Aragorn, high qualities more often associated with the Elves are softened and humanized.

Because of his ancient Númenorian ancestry, Aragon's lifespan far exceeds that of normal humans; in fact he lives for 210 years, ruling for 120 of those years as King of Gondor. This increased lifespan is important to the plot of *The Lord of the Rings*, where much is made of Aragorn's longevity as the last flowering of the Númenoreans. The fan fiction movie, *Born of Hope*, directed by Kate

Madison, tells the story of Aragorn's parents, Arathorn and Gilraen, based on Appendixes in *The Lord of the Rings*, which provide 'historical background' to the War of the Ring. This movie can be viewed freely at www.bornofhope.com.

ARAGORN'S NAMES

Frodo Baggins and his Hobbit companions first come across Aragorn under the name of Strider at Bree. In Tolkien's early drafts, the character Strider has the name of Trotter, and is a brown-faced Hobbit wearing clattering clogs rather than a stealthy hero of Númenor. When disguised as Strider, Aragorn is a Ranger, a name given to those of the lost kingdom of Arnor who guard The Shire and the larger region of Eriador. Yet as heir to the kingship, he is in fact their leader; indeed after his coronation, Aragorn is named King Elessar. As a youth in Rivendell, he is disguised by the name Estel, meaning 'hope'; one of his ancient names is Envinyatar, the Renewer, owing to his healing powers. Other names of Aragorn's include Thorongil, Isildur's Heir, the Renewer, Longshanks and Wing-foot.

Viggo Mortensen, who played Aragorn in Peter Jackson's film

Gothmog, Lord of the Balrogs, riding a dragon.

Do Balrogs have wings?
*The perennial debate
of the fandom*

There is a legend that medieval thinkers enjoyed debating how many angels could dance on the point of a pin. The question about Balrogs' wings could be a little like this: pointless fun that may, in the future, be used to debunk the fans of J.R.R. Tolkien. Yet, the debate about angels actually hints at a more serious debate that has raged over

the millennia: whether angels have a body that occupies space – certainly if they did, it is unlikely that even one could dance on a needle. Meanwhile, the debate about Balrogs arises from an ambiguity in Tolkien's descriptions of these magical creatures, which he developed over the more than 50 years he spent shaping his mythology of Middle-earth.

Balrogs in Tolkien mythology are demons of fire that served Morgoth, his equivalent of Satan. Their name is Elvish in origin, meaning 'Demon of Might'. Balrogs are a type of lesser angelic power known as the Maiar but turned renegade, and carry whips of flame. Such beings could take on real physical form, as did the wizard Gandalf, also of the Maiar. The Balrog killed by Gandalf in *The Lord of the Rings* was so ancient that it had survived the destruction of Morgoth's stronghold in the long-ago First Age of Middle-earth. Tolkien's fertile imagination created or utilized many embodiments of evil such as Balrogs, dragons, orcs, the fallen Morgoth and his servant Sauron, ringwraiths, monster spiders such as Shelob or Ungoliant, werewolves and trolls.

So, what about the wings?

The Lord of the Rings records how the Company of the Ring disturbed a Balrog deep underneath Khazad-dûm, in the underground realm of Moria, and how Gandalf sacrificed his life fighting the monster. In Tolkien's description of this event, there is a hint that the Balrog might have wings of some sort, for the company saw its shadow stretching 'like two vast wings'. However, unlike the Balrog's body, those wings may not have been made of flesh and blood but rather of some sort of dense shadow. This is why, when the Balrog is in front of the fissure of fire, the fire seems overcast as by a cloud rather than eclipsed. If the Balrog does indeed have wings, it appears these do not have the substance of its physical body. Thus, the debate about Balrogs' wings can continue indefinitely, rather like the debate on the space that angels occupy.

There is something satisfying in Balrogs not having corporeal wings, which means that the Balrog whom Gandalf fought would eventually hit the bottom of the great chasm with a colossal, well-earned thwack. But this leaves the question: how did the monster survive the great fall? We are told that Gandalf pursued his dire enemy until, over a month later, he followed it right to the height of Zirak-zigil, in the mountain chain above Moria, before throwing the monster down to his death and then dying himself.

Let there be dragons
J.R.R. Tolkien's desire for monsters

As a child, J.R.R. Tolkien admitted: 'I desired dragons…' It was the retelling of the story of Sigurd slaying the dragon Fáfnir in Andrew Lang's *Red Fairy Book* that truly fired his youthful imagination. At around the age of six or seven Tolkien wrote about a 'green great dragon'. His mother told him that the correct order of saying this was 'a great green dragon', and years later, as an eminent Professor of English language at Oxford, he still couldn't find a reason why this should be so. After his death, his adult retelling from Old Norse of Sigurd and Fáfnir, a story he had always loved, was eventually published.

Tolkien's stories of Middle-earth over the Ages, leading up to the time of the destruction of Sauron's Ring, reveal a kind of dragon lore or history. Morgoth, Tolkien's Satan equivalent, probably bred dragons. In early Ages, dragons could not fly; even later, the dragons called cold-drakes apparently could not breathe out fire. Dragons were always, however, malevolent and capable of beguiling speech. Tolkien owed much to northern European imagination in his depiction of these beasts, including the way the scaly creatures greedily hoarded treasure. Early dragons participated in the fall of the hidden Elven city of Gondor; metal dragons that carried orcs and were built by Morgoth also took part in that great battle. One of the greatest and most feared dragons of the early Ages of Middle-earth was Glaurung, who was killed by Túrin Turambar in one of Tolkien's best but unfinished stories, *The Children of Húrin* (2007).

The dragon Smaug

Smaug is at the centre of the plot of *The Hobbit*, and is the last of the great dragons of Middle-earth, although some lesser ones apparently remain at the time of *The Lord of the Rings* and beyond. Smaug's conversational manner with Bilbo Baggins is modelled partly on that of Fáfnir in the northern myth. After *The Hobbit*, evil is embodied mainly in Sauron's lost Ring carried by Frodo, rather than in a dragon or any other living monster. Dragons in European imagination are linked to the haunting portrayal of Satan in the Book of Revelation; yet, in *The Lord of the Rings* devilry takes on a modern form, in the Ring that is a machine created by the Dark Lord.

The mysterious Tom Bombadil
Spirit of the Berkshire and Oxfordshire countryside?

Tom Bombadil is an enigmatic figure in *The Lord of the Rings*, with a powerful appeal to the imagination. As a nature spirit living in the Old Forest east of The Shire, he is mastered by none and refuses possession himself. J.R.R. Tolkien was uncertain of this character's status, but it is possible that Tom is one of the Maiar, the lesser angelic beings. Indeed, we are told that he is 'Master of wood, water and hill' and in a letter to his publisher in 1937, Tolkien speaks of Tom as the spirit of the vanishing countryside of Berkshire and Oxfordshire. Tom tells the Hobbits that he has been in the location of the forest from before the river and the trees; that he has observed the very first raindrop and the first acorn; and that, in the earliest days of Middle-earth when the Elves awoke, Tom was already there.

'Tom Bombadil' is the name given to him by Hobbits; Elves, dwarves and men know him by other names. Like the biblical Adam, Tom is himself a name-giver. When he bestows names upon the Hobbits' ponies, the animals answer to them 'for the rest of their lives'. There is a comic, almost Hobbit-like description of him in the collection of verses *The Adventures of Tom Bombadil*; he has affinities with Puck, the spirit of English nature, especially in Rudyard Kipling's portrayal in his book *Puck of Pook's Hill* (1906). Like the wizards in *The Lord of the Rings*, Tom appears like a man although, unlike Gandalf and the

Puck, the spirit of English nature

others, he is a comic, colourful figure, dressed in a bright blue jacket and yellow boots. His songs have power over nature, and even his speech has no distinction between prose and poetry.

One of Tom's functions in *The Lord of the Rings* is to provide a perspective on the vast Ages of Middle-earth before the War of the Rings, right back to the beginning of creation. Tom's character also provides a sharp contrast to the pursuit of power, epitomized by the Dark Lord and symbolized in the One Ring, which holds no power over him.

Talking creatures
Gods and goddesses and nymphs and Elves

Talking creatures have a long tradition in literature, mythology and folk tales. Aesop's ancient fables, which feature such beasts, are still read today. C.S. Lewis's Narnia, a land of talking animals, is immensely popular throughout the world; talking creatures are also to be found in Lewis' science fiction stories. There are further examples of talking animals in contemporary fantasy such as the great armoured bear, Iorek Byrnison, in Philip Pullman's *Northern Lights* (1995).

J.R.R. Tolkien has many such creatures in his stories, from the hound Huan in the tale of Beren and Lúthien in *The Silmarillion*, to Smaug the dragon in *The Hobbit*, and Gwaihir, Lord of the Eagles, in *The Lord of the Rings*. He also has talking trees, the Ents, taking the principle of something human-like embodied in an animal to further extremes as vegetation. Many forms of life in Tolkien's stories have a spiritual awareness and a consciousness that is human, in that they are rational and use language; indeed, even the foul orcs are talking beings. At the other end of the spectrum are the Elves, who are immortal and more spiritually developed than other races. They have bodies genetically compatible with, and beautiful in the eyes of, humans.

Sub-creation
Lewis regarded the invention of talking creatures as a feature of what Tolkien called 'sub-creation'; that

Treebeard, the Ent

is, when we make other worlds containing magical creatures like talking animals we are, in effect, 'sub-creators', creating in God's image. What Lewis once wrote can be seen as a commentary on Tolkien's idea: 'We do not want merely to see beauty…We want something else which can hardly be put into words—to be united with the beauty we see, to pass into it, to receive it into ourselves, to bathe in it, to become part of it. That is why we have peopled air and earth and water with gods and goddesses and nymphs and Elves.' One might add to Lewis' examples some of the other talking creatures of *The Silmarillion*, *The Hobbit*, and *The Lord of the Rings* such as Ents, wizards and eagles. Talking creatures that have deformed their beauty by wickedness, or have been purpose-built for evil, serve as contrast to goodness; for example, dragons, orcs and Sauron himself.

Talking creatures at one time were limited to children's books, such as *The Wind in the Willows*, by Kenneth Grahame, or the tales of Beatrix Potter. Both Tolkien and his friend C.S. Lewis created talking beings suitable for an adult readership, drawing on a rich tradition from ancient storytellers.

The eagles are coming!
The eternal hope of Middle-earth

At the darkest moment in the War of the Ring, when all seems lost for the army of the West, Gandalf looks to the sky and cries, 'The eagles are coming!' They arrive to help in the fight and just as they do, the One Ring is destroyed deep in Mordor.

Eagles play an important part in the events of Middle-earth over the Ages, and are associated with the protective acts and judgment of Ilúvatar, the creator of all, and his angelic servants known as the Valar. The eagles are noble, enormous creatures – the wingspan of the great eagle Thorondor is 180ft (55m) – and are large enough to carry Hobbits and even men. They protect the ancient Elven city of Gondolin, then help Tuor and the other survivors after its fall; they rescue the lovers Beren and Lúthien after they steal back a precious Silmaril from the iron crown of Morgoth; and they assist in the

Manwë of the Valar ordained that eagles nest in mountains, not in high trees, so that they could hear and report to him when the voices of men and Elves called to him for help. Of the Valar, Manwë had the greatest understanding of the will and designs of Ilúvatar. He was particularly associated with air, clouds and the wind, and with the birds of the air, especially the eagles.

BIRDS OF MIDDLE-EARTH

Middle-earth is teeming with wildlife, yet a number of birds are featured in particular: eagles, crows and crow-like birds called the crebain, ravens, thrushes, swans, and nightingales. Roäc is the chief of the friendly ravens of the Lonely Mountain in **The Hobbit,** *and informs Thorin of Smaug's death at Lake-town. Also in* **The Hobbit,** *an old thrush passes on to Bard the Bowman a tip regarding the dragon's weak spot noticed by Bilbo, which allows Bard's arrow to penetrate the gap in the beast's scaly armour. The wizard Radagast is responsible for the welfare of animals, and is particularly*

fight against winged dragons at the end of the First Age.

In the Second Age of Middle-earth, eagle-shaped clouds presage the destruction of the western island of Númenor. In later times during the Third Age, eagles aid Bilbo Baggins and Thorin's dwarves in the events leading up to the death of the dragon Smaug, especially during the Battle of the Five Armies. Furthermore the great eagle, Gwaihir the Windlord, rescues Frodo and his companion Sam from the burning slopes of Mount Doom after the destruction of the Ring.

friendly with birds; the renegade wizard Saruman contemptuously calls him the 'bird-tamer'.

Dwarves
But not the Disney sort

In J.R.R. Tolkien's Middle-earth, dwarves are one of the free peoples, therefore directly given life by Ilúvatar, maker of all, rather than being brought into existence by his angelic agents, the Valar. In actual fact Aulë of the Valar shaped them, but could not give them personal life; although the dwarves are not his direct concept, Ilúvatar takes pity on Aulë and brings life to what his servant has formed.

Designed by Aulë to resist the evils of Morgoth, dwarves are short and hardy; and although proud, they withstand evil. Like their shaper Aulë, dwarves are drawn to the substances of the earth – metals, minerals and precious stones – and they are masters of craft. Dwarves have their own secret language, and a great and constant temptation for them is to possess. They live long lives, not marrying as a rule until they are 100 years old.

In *The Hobbit*, Bilbo Baggins travels with a party of 13 dwarves, Thorin and Company, to seek the dragon's treasure that had once belonged to their kin. The dwarves employ Bilbo Baggins as their burglar to steal it, at the recommendation of the wizard, Gandalf the Grey. In *The Lord of the Rings*, the dwarf Gimli is a member of the Company of the Ring; his friendship with Legolas the Elf helps to heal an ancient enmity between the two races.

Dwarves also play an important role in the Ages of Middle-earth leading up to the time of *The Hobbit*. Nauglamir, or the Necklace of the Dwarves, plays a role in *The Silmarillion*. Set with many jewels, the necklace was made for the eminent Elf, Finrod Felagund, by dwarves. In a later period, King Thingol hires dwarves to refashion it, setting in it a Silmaril, the precious gem of light that Beren and Lúthien wrestled from the Satanic Morgoth.

DWARFS OR DWARVES?

Tolkien preferred the plural 'dwarves' to the dictionary–orthodox plural 'dwarfs', so he was annoyed when the typesetters of the first volume of **The Lord of the Rings** *in 1953 corrected his 'dwarves' to 'dwarfs'; this resulted in a large number of tedious corrections to his set of galley proofs. Tolkien believed the plural in English should really have been 'dwarrows', had it developed properly. His use of 'dwarves' was also intended to help to distance the diminutive beings from 'the sillier tales' where they were often figures of fun – as, presumably, in Disney's seven 'dwarfs', Sneezy, Dopey, Grumpy, Doc and the rest.*

Little fairies and large Elves
Tolkien shifts to adult readers

In J.R.R. Tolkien's early writings, his fairy beings are those favoured in Victorian times, and also found in the writings of Shakespeare and others: tiny creatures, often with fluttering wings, who dwell in flowers. Such ideas of fairies were still very much the vogue in the early twentieth century. Indeed, a popular fairy play at the time was J.M. Barrie's *Peter Pan*, which Tolkien saw in Birmingham as an 18-year-old; Tinkerbell, the famous fairy from the story, effectively sums up the Victorian image of such beings. One of Tolkien's early poems was

John Anster Fitzgerald's The Captive Robin

called *Wood-sunshine*, in which he wrote of 'light fairy things' who were 'All fashion'd of radiance, careless of grief.'

The way he imagined fairies, or Fair Folk, then was very different from his mature depiction of them in the form of Elves in *The Lord of the Rings* and *The Silmarillion*, books both aimed at adult readers. Tolkien began to regard with distaste the idea of Elves and fairy folk as dainty, diminutive figures and from then on, he was to depict Elves without wings, yet physically larger than humans, and spiritually superior. His mature portrayal of Elves is inspired by older literature and stories that long predated Shakespeare, such as *Beowulf* and other tales from northern mythology.

In his letters, Tolkien describes the mythology of Middle-earth as being 'Elf-centred'; this is embodied in *The Silmarillion*, which largely concerns the First Age of Middle-earth. The Elvish framework of *The Silmarillion* is particularly evident when compared to *The Hobbit* and *The Lord of the Rings*; both latter titles could be described as Hobbit-centred, the narrative being composed from the point of view of Hobbits who are a form of human being.

Tolkien's Elves are, like mankind, the Children of Ilúvatar, maker of all; they are not part of the creation fashioned by the Valar, his angelic servants. The Elves awake to life by the shores of a bay called Cuiviénen, but soon divide into two groups: the Eldar, who take part in the great journey to the utter West at the summons of the Valar; and those who refuse the call, including the Sindar. The two main variants of their language, Quenya and Sindarin, develop from this division.

The First Age of Middle-earth is the golden age of the Elves who remain in Middle-earth. In the latter Ages, they are a remnant who gather in localized Elven-realms. As they fade in splendour and influence, mankind gradually becomes ascendant. Elves resemble mankind and can marry them, as did the Elf-maiden Lúthien with Beren. However they are normally immortal and tied, even should they die, to this world; those who marry humans must choose to renounce their immortality for the mortality of their human partners.

GOBLIN'S FEET

*The first mainstream publication of Tolkien's literary work was in **Oxford Poetry 1915**; his contribution, entitled 'Goblin Feet', was subsequently published in various collections. He had written these verses in the spring of 1915, and they featured tiny fairy goblins with lamps and flying 'flittermice' among the flowers and trees at dusk. It transpired that he wrote these verses to please his fiancée, Edith Bratt, who delighted in flower fairies.*

Do Elves have pointed ears?
Exploring the scant evidence

Apparently, neither *The Hobbit* nor *The Lord of the Rings* makes any mention of Elves, nor indeed Hobbits, having pointed ears. Nevertheless, anyone who has seen Peter Jackson's movies of these stories will know that this is how they are visualized.

In his mind's eye, however, J.R.R. Tolkien did see both Elves and Hobbits as having pointed ears. The evidence must be delved as assiduously as dwarves mine silver. In a letter to his US publisher about his illustrations for *The Hobbit*, Tolkien wrote of drawing his Hobbits with 'ears only slightly pointed and "Elvish"'. Elsewhere, in an unfinished piece of writing he writes of Elf-ears being 'pointed and leaf-shaped'.

Their own ears

Fans of Tolkien often enjoy dressing up in Elvish or Hobbitish garb, which naturally, they believe, requires pointed ears. An enthusiast for Tolkien's writings – whom we shall not name, to spare his blushes – was queuing for the autographs of leading Tolkien artists, John Howe and Alan Lee; meanwhile two women in front of him were wearing fetching Elven costumes. They were delighted when he complimented them on their costumes and asked if they had made the clothes. However their smiles turned to frost when he queried how they had managed to blend the colour of their commendable ears so well with their own skin tones; he suffered an icy silence from him for the next two hours in the queue. As you've guessed, the ears were their own.

Gandalf the Grey
There's more to a wizard than meets the eye

Sir Ian McKellen, who played Gandalf in Peter Jackson's film

Gandalf is one of the two most well known of the wizards, the other being Saruman, whose lust for power eventually corrupts him. In *The Hobbit* and *The Lord of the Rings*, Gandalf appears as an old man and a great wizard. In fact, he is one of the Maiar, the lesser angelic powers, and was sent by the Valar, the principal angelic powers, to Middle-earth to assist those who opposed the evil of Sauron. In his youth spent in Valinor, the land of the angelic powers in the utter West, he was called Olórin; he also had many other names such as Mithrandir, Tharkûn, Grey Pilgrim, and Stormcrow.

Only a small number of beings, including the Elven princess Galadriel, know the origins of the five or so wizards. They appeared in Middle-earth around the year 1000 of the Third Age, at the time when the shadow and menace of Sauron, a renegade power, began to reappear. The wizards were subsequently sent as emissaries from the Valar to encourage resistance to Sauron. Capable of error and failure, and of experiencing great pain because they had taken on physical bodies, they could be killed; furthermore, the power of the One Ring affected them.

The three wizard agents in *The Lord of the Rings* are Saruman the White, Gandalf the Grey, and Radagast the Brown. Another two wizards, Alatar and Pallando, are collectively known as the Ithryn Luin, or the Blue Wizards, in Tolkien's *Unfinished Tales*. They had the role of 'missionaries to enemy occupied lands', far away from the familiar lands that are the setting of *The Lord of the Rings*. Typically, in a letter Tolkien writes of his suspicion that the Blue Wizards failed in the quest the Valinor set them, as had Saruman by embracing evil. He suspected that these wizards were founders of secret cults and 'magic' traditions that persisted into the Fourth Age.

Faithful to his calling as a wizard, Gandalf is a prime protagonist in the fight against Sauron. On his coronation, Aragorn states of Gandalf that 'he has been the mover of all that has been accomplished, and this is his victory'. Gandalf is also important because he interprets the providence of events. For example, he reveals the key role that the pity of Frodo and Sam for Gollum played; he also foresees what can be accomplished by the 'foolish' act of sending weak Hobbits into the stronghold of Sauron to destroy the Ring.

Gandalf was a Ring-bearer. He wore Narya, the Ring of Fire, which was also called the Kindler; he represents this powerful aspect of himself in a childlike way to the Hobbits as a love of fireworks.

Gandalf declares himself the servant of the Secret Fire, which lies at the heart of all that is good in Middle-earth.

THE MAIAR

In **The Silmarillion,** *the Maiar are angelic beings, of lesser degree than the Valar; they steward and guard the world under the direction of the Valar, and are capable of various incarnations. Those who remain loyal to the Valar and Ilúvatar include Olórin (Gandalf), the Elven Queen Melian, and most likely Tom Bombadil; the Maiar who rebel express degrees of depravity and include Sauron, once striking in appearance, and the Balrogs.*

Galadriel, the Elven princess
Linking past and present events in Middle-earth

In J.R.R. Tolkien's mythology Galadriel is an Elven princess, born in the First Age of Middle-earth. She is one of the greatest of the Elves, strong-willed and brilliant, whose moral character develops and matures over the Ages. As an immortal, she is active in significant events over a vast period of history before the role she plays in *The Lord of the Rings*, thereby acting as a strong linking force throughout the stories. Galadriel's name in Sindarin Elvish means 'Maiden crowned with gleaming hair'. She is given this name in her youth because she has long hair, which glistens with gold but is also diffused with silver. At that time, her disposition was like that of an Amazon warrior and when she took part in athletic events, she bound up her hair as a crown.

Galadriel is implicated in the rebellion against the Valar of the Elves skilled in craftsmanship and of great knowledge, called the Noldor. Hence, she is forbidden to return to Valinor, the Undying Lands of the uttermost West. The Valar only relent and let her return at the end of the Third Age, following the destruction of the Ring. In ancient days, she lives on a green river island before moving to the great Elven kingdom of Doriath. In this largely wooded kingdom she is taught by the wise Queen Melian, the mother of Lúthien whose love of the human Beren is one of the greatest stories of Middle-earth. Galadriel is to model on Doriath her realm of Lothlórien (also called simply Lórien), which lies to the east of the Misty Mountains.

It is in Doriath, in one version of her story, that Galadriel marries Celeborn, whom the Ringbearer Frodo Baggins and his companions are to meet in the distant future. After the destruction of a large northwestern area of Middle-earth called Beleriand, which includes Doriath, Galadriel eventually lives for a while in Eregion to the west of the Misty Mountains, before founding Lórien in the Second Age. By this time she has become keeper of Nenya, one of the Elven Rings, also known as the Ring of Water. The *Unfinished Tales*, compiled after Tolkien's death by his son Christopher Tolkien, includes an account of the history of Galadriel and Celeborn, which speaks of the origin of the Elessar, the brooch eventually bequeathed to Aragorn by Arwen, Galadriel's granddaughter. It also provides some additional details of Galadriel's history over the Ages.

A significant moral moment in Galadriel's tale is her temptation when offered the One Ring by Frodo Baggins in *The Lord of the Rings*: she contemplates the possibility of successfully wielding the Ring against Sauron, the Dark Lord. Indeed, it is her resistance to the lure of power that leads the Valar to reverse their ban and allow her to return to Valinor. The Elven princess has a constant desire for the undying lands of Valinor, and this longing is fulfilled when she is allowed to return with the other Ring-bearers at the end of *The Lord of the Rings*.

The gift of Galadriel

Of great significance to the plot of *The Lord of the Rings* is a crystal jar that Galadriel bequeaths as a gift to Frodo known as the Phial of Galadriel. The jar contains the light of Eärendil, a star known to us as the planet Venus, the Morning or Evening Star, whose light was captured in the Mirror of Galadriel. Because of its source, light from the Phial brings hope and courage to a bearer who has faith. With the Phial, Frodo is able to

resist the attraction of the Ring, and his loyal companion Sam is able to confront Shelob, the grotesque giant spider. The Phial has a sacramental value in the unfolding story, hinting at a deeper reality and a magical power behind the world.

THE THREE RINGS

These were the Three Rings of Power belonging to the Elves. Although made without Sauron's help, the ruling One Ring in which his power was stored could control them. When the One Ring was destroyed in the Cracks of Doom, the Three Rings lost their power. Unlike the other Rings – seven Rings for the Dwarves, ten for mortal men, and the ruling Ring – their power did not lie in control and domination because Sauron's hand was not in their making; rather, their power lay in building, understanding and healing. The Three Rings were called Vilya, Nenya and Narya; Elrond of Rivendell wore Vilya, Galadriel wore Nenya and Gandalf wore Narya.

Dark-loving orcs
The race bred for evil

Orcs are a race bred by Morgoth, J.R.R. Tolkien's Satan figure, to carry out his evil; as beings, they thus have no moral choice. Yet even as some kind of biological robot, they do have an advanced consciousness. Morgoth was incapable of creating life, so for his genetic engineering he apparently made use of captured Elves that he had tortured. While the Elves symbolize what is high and noble in human life, the orcs represent what is base, twisted, insensitive and cruel. Orcs have different names in various languages; for example, Hobbits call them goblins.

Morgoth made use of orcs as far back as the First Age in his attempts to dominate and suppress Beleriand, the ancient land of Middle-earth eventually engulfed by sea. After Morgoth's downfall and the destruction of Beleriand, orcs survived in other parts of Middle-earth; in the Second and Third Ages, Sauron, who had served Morgoth, uses them in his oppressive forces.

There are various types and tribes of orcs, not all loyal to Sauron as some serve Saruman. A later type of orc, especially bred as a warrior being in the Third Age by Sauron, is the Uruk-hai or Great Orc (singular uruk, plural uruks). By the period of the War of the Ring, both Sauron and the treacherous wizard Saruman employ uruks as soldiers; Frodo and Sam encounter uruks including Gorbag and Shagrat in Mordor. Sauron bred uruks to be taller than the usual orc, nearly as tall as humans; in addition, they did not weaken in sunlight like the dark-loving orcs.

BLACK SPEECH

The orcs of Mordor use a debased form of Black Speech. Devised by Sauron in the Second Age and revived by him in the Third Age, this may be a perverted form of Quenya or high Elvish. An example of pure Black Speech is the inscription on the One Ring in **The Lord of the Rings.**

Giant spiders
A monstrous enemy

As a toddler in South Africa, J.R.R. Tolkien was bitten by a tarantula, yet later denied a link between this childhood experience and the prevalence of bloated, giant spiders in Middle-earth. Indeed, he claimed no particular fear of anachrids. Nevertheless in Tolkien's stories, monstrous spiders, like dragons, symbolize an enemy of humankind far greater than death. The courage of Sam Gamgee the Hobbit against the monstrous Shelob in her dark lair is a notable example; in this encounter, Sam faced no ordinary danger but something paralyzingly dreadful. The heroes of ancient tales visit underground places to face necessary terrors; Shelob's lair is but one such place in Tolkien's Middle-earth.

Shelob – her name a combination of 'she' and an Old English word for spider, 'lob' – is an ancient creature from the First Age of Middle-earth, spawned by her even more terrifying mother Ungoliant, who poisoned the lights which originally illuminated the undying lands of the Valar. *The Silmarillion* tells how Ungoliant, with the renegade member of the Valar, Morgoth, destroys the Two Trees that lit up Valinor. Ungoliant may have been one of the fallen Maiar or lesser angelic powers, who had taken on a spider-like form that swelled hideously as a result of her greed.

PREDATOR FROM HELL

In the Third Age of Middle-earth, Shelob was 'the last child of Ungoliant to trouble the unhappy world'. She had escaped the destruction of Beleriand in what had been the northwest of Middle-earth and subsequently made her way south. Creating her den in the mountain pass of Cirith Ungol, she preyed on humans, Elves and orcs, thus guarding that route into Mordor. Gollum treacherously led Frodo Baggins and his companion Sam into her Lair, but Sam managed to blind Shelob, aided by the Phial given to Frodo by Galadriel to use in such a time.

J.R.R. TOLKIEN, SCHOLAR AND WRITER

The Silmarillion
Backdrop to The Hobbit *and* The Lord of the Rings

There are two manifestations of J.R.R. Tolkien's 'the Silmarillion'. One is the published volume, *The Silmarillion* (1977), edited by Tolkien's son Christopher, with the assistance of writer Guy Kay, which appeared four years after Tolkien's death. The other is a body of stories, poems, lexicons, annals, reflections, genealogies, maps and illustrations on the early Ages of Middle-earth and its universe, composed by Tolkien over nearly 60 years. To this second body can also be added the many letters that Tolkien wrote explaining various aspects of his invented world.

While the focus of both these manifestations is the precious gems of light known as the Silmarils and the First Age of Middle-earth, they also describe the beginnings of the world, and the Ages that followed the First Age. In fact, this larger focus embraces the origin, history and fate of the Elves of Middle-earth, into which is tied a complex mythology reflecting orthodox Christian theology.

The Silmarillion

The Silmarillion, the published volume, is a continuous narrative skilfully selected from the vast body of Tolkien's unfinished work. It is not intended to suggest a finished work, but does provide an authorative and relatively accessible framework for fitting together the wider material. The unfinished nature of Tolkien's writings about the early history of Middle-earth is most evident in several important tales that are contained in *The Silmarillion*: the stories of Beren and Lúthien the Elf-maiden, Túrin Turambar, Tuor and the Fall of Gondolin, and Eärendil the mariner. In some cases, these are quite condensed versions; they might one day have appeared on a more expanded scale had Tolkien completed them.

The summary nature of much of *The Silmarillion* can initially prove difficult reading for those new to it. This difficulty is compounded by a deluge of unfamiliar names faced even by readers who are familiar with *The Hobbit* and *The Lord of the Rings*. Indeed, when J.E.A. Tyler updated his *Tolkien Companion* to include *The Silmarillion* it was necessary for him to add about 1,800 new entries.

The Silmarillion is divided into several sections. The first is the 'Ainulindalë', the Elves' beautiful account of the creation of the world. The second section is the 'Valaquenta', the history of the Valar or angelic powers. Then follows the main and largest section, the 'Quenta Silmarillion', translating as the 'history of the Silmarils', which is the Silmarillion proper as its focus is on the Silmarils, the precious jewels of light. The fourth section is the 'Akallabêth', the account of the Downfall of the island kingdom of Númenor. Then the final section, 'Of the Rings of Power and the Third Age', concerns the history of the Rings of Power, including the Great Ring, and of the Third Age of Middle-earth leading to the events described in *The Lord of the Rings*.

It would seem that Tolkien intended all these sections to eventually appear in revised form in one volume, thus setting out his mythology of Middle-earth comprehensively. He comments at length upon the development of the history of Middle-earth through the Three Ages in a enormously long letter to a publisher, which is usefully published at the beginning of a later paperback edition of *The Silmarillion* (1999).

The wider material

The second Silmarillion is the entire body of unfinished material left by Tolkien at his death, which exists in poetry as well as prose. The material indicates the author's desire to create an interconnected body of legends, now become known by scholars as his 'legendarium'. Much of this wide body of material has been published since his death, edited and commentated upon by his son, Christopher. This work can be found in books such as J.R.R. Tolkien's *Unfinished Tales of Númenor and Middle-earth* or the twelve volumes of his *The History of Middle-earth*.

The story of Farmer Giles
A giant, a blunderbuss, and a dragon

Farmer Giles of Ham is a light-hearted short story which is, on the surface, of interest to children, yet is full of the playfulness of a master of language. It is set before the days of King Arthur in the valley of the Thames. Its fictional setting, the Little Kingdom, has similarities with The Shire, particularly in the sheltered and homely life of the village of Ham. The story's protagonist, Farmer Giles, resembles a complacent Hobbit in all but size, with unexpected qualities.

One night a rather deaf and short-sighted giant wanders by mistake near Giles' farm, trampling his fields and animals. The nervous farmer lets fly with a blunderbuss stuffed with wire, stones, and other debris. The giant, not hearing the bang, supposes himself stung and quickly leaves that place with its apparently unpleasant horseflies. Farmer Giles is now the village hero; even the King of the Little Kingdom hears of his deed and sends him the gift of a long sword.

The farmer enjoys his reputation in peace until a dragon comes to hear of the rich kingdom from the giant. Times being hard, Chrysophylax Dives (for that was the dragon's name) comes to investigate the Little Kingdom. The dragon makes a nuisance of himself, but the King's knights prove unwilling to take him on; meanwhile, the scaly creature gets closer and closer to Ham. It turns out that the sword given to Giles is called Tailbiter and had belonged to a renowned dragon-slayer. The pressure was naturally on for the reluctant hero to go dragon hunting, so with Garm his dog, and his old grey mare, the farmer sets off.

Much to Giles' surprise, the wily dragon greets him with a 'Good morning', his next meal very much on his mind. However, the sword Tailbiter nonplusses the dragon with good reason for, after challenging the dragon, Farmer Giles wounds the dragon's wing, thus rendering him unable to fly. The dragon starts to run away, pursued by the fat farmer on his grey mare, with the good folk of Ham cheering the pursuit. Eventually the exhausted dragon bargains to

St Peter and St Paul's Church, Worminghall

save his skin: if Farmer Giles will let him return home, the dragon would eventually return with treasure. Giles agrees and the dragon leaves for home in the far off mountains, with no intention of returning. The day soon arrives when the dragon had agreed to return, but of course he doesn't.

Giles makes his way with his mare and dog to the mountains where the dragon lives, carrying his eager sword. Frightened of Tailbiter, the dragon is forced to load the treasure onto his back and return it. From that time, Farmer Giles was Lord of the region around the village, backed up by his tamed dragon – or tame worm, to use an old word for dragon – who was housed in a 'hall', or barn. Giles became known as Lord of the Tame Worm, and eventually Lord of Tame. This title led to the name, Thame, as

Ham and Tame became conflated. The humbled dragon was eventually allowed by Giles to return home to the mountains.

This humorous story, although on the surface very different from the tales of Middle-earth, is nevertheless characteristic of J.R.R. Tolkien in its themes. The story's inspiration is linguistic, providing a spoof explanation for the name of an actual village east of Oxford called Worminghall, near Thame.

The Adventures of Tom Bombadil
From Dutch doll to literary celebrity

Published in 1961, *The Adventures of Tom Bombadil* is a collection of light and sometimes nonsense verses deriving, we are led to believe, from the pages of *The Red Book of Westmarch*, a fictional book containing Bilbo Baggins' account of the events in *The Hobbit* and *The Lord of the Rings*. The verses are supposedly written by Bilbo, along with Frodo Baggins, Sam Gamgee, and other Hobbits; they are 'translated' by J.R.R.

Tolkien, who adds an explanatory note, and illustrated by Pauline Baynes. Largely relating the legends and jests of The Shire at the end of the Third Age, Tolkien's talent for songs, ballads and witty riddles suits this Hobbitish setting well.

The collection is named after a major piece in it, one of three poems concerning Tom Bombadil's adventures, which beautifully reveal the character's affinity with nature. It was first published in 1934 in the *Oxford Magazine*, inspired by a Dutch doll belonging to Tolkien's infant son Michael, which had a splendid feather in its hat. This was before Tolkien had even conceived of *The Lord of the Rings*; nevertheless, the character Tom Bombadil was eventually drawn into that story.

The Nobel Prize
Tolkien's failure in this arena

In 1961, J.R.R. Tolkien failed to be awarded the Nobel Prize in Literature; amazingly, his epic *The Lord of the Rings* was deemed second rate. Indeed, it has now been revealed that the jury concluded that his work had 'not in any way measured up to storytelling of the highest quality'. The winner, the Yugoslav writer Ivo Andric, was selected from a list of around 50 writers whose names had been nominated by leading academics, experts and winners from former years; Tolkien's name had been put forward by his great friend C.S. Lewis, who taught literature at Oxford University.

According to the jury, the Nobel Prize in Literature that year was awarded to Ivo Andric 'for the epic force with which he has traced themes and depicted human destinies drawn from the history of his country'. Nonetheless, in failing to win the Prize Tolkien found himself in distinguished company: others on the Nobel list who had failed ultimate selection for the Prize included E.M. Forster, author of *Howard's End*, Lawrence Durrell, who wrote *The Alexandria Quartet,* and Graham Greene, writer of *Brighton Rock, The End of the Affair* and many other novels. Yet more who can be added to this distinguished list include the US poet Robert Frost, the Danish writer Karen Blixen,

and Italy's Alberto Moravia.

C.S. Lewis clearly thought that Tolkien was a storyteller of the highest order, a verdict shared by millions of readers around the globe. Lewis was widely read in fiction of all periods, including the Middle Ages, a primary source of Tolkien's inspiration for fantasy. On 7 January 1961 Lewis wrote in confidence to a brilliant former student of his at Oxford, seeking advice: 'If you were asked to nominate a candidate for the Nobel Prize (literature) who wd. be your choice?…Frost? Eliot? Tolkien? E.M. Forster?…Keep this all under your hat.' C.S. Lewis in the end decided upon Tolkien.

Professionally fruitful
J.R.R. Tolkien at the University of Leeds

The University of Leeds was founded in 1904, just 16 years prior to J.R.R. Tolkien's arrival as Reader in English Language. Its English Department was developing extensively under Professor George S. Gordon, who had come from Oxford University for this purpose.

Gordon introduced to the university the Oxford English School syllabus, in which students could choose between some specialist courses in medieval English language and literature, or 'modern' literature after Chaucer.

On Tolkien's arrival at Leeds in 1921, Gordon allowed him to form a School of English Philology within the English Department and Tolkien was inspired by the challenge. It wasn't long before a much larger number of students than usual were taking specialist courses on English language. Tolkien, along with his colleague E.V. Gordon, also formed the Viking Club for their students. Amongst other pastimes, members of this club were able to enjoy translating nursery rhymes into Anglo-Saxon and singing rowdy drinking songs in Old Norse.

By 1924, at the age of 32 years old, Tolkien was a youthful Professor of English Language at the university. Furthermore, with E.V. Gordon he was preparing an edition of *Sir Gawain and the Green Knight* that would be used widely and is still in print as an edition revised by Norman Davis, nearly 90 years later. By the

The Great Hall, University of Leeds

next year, he had been appointed Rawlinson and Bosworth Professor of Anglo-Saxon at Oxford.

Those five years at Leeds were professionally fruitful. They were also a happy time for Tolkien and his growing family, during which they holidayed in Yorkshire locations such as Filey on the east coast. In Leeds, they lived at various addresses, finding their way eventually to a large house in Darnley Road, which in those days had open fields nearby in which the children could walk.

Saved from disaster
Tolkien at Exeter College, Oxford

J.R.R. Tolkien was an undergraduate at Oxford University's Exeter College in Turl Street from 1911 to 1915. Walter de Stapeldon, who became Bishop of Exeter, founded the college in 1314. Indeed, the name of the college reflects the West Country origins of its founder, and during its early centuries of existence college members were sourced mainly from the West Country locations of Cornwall and Devon.

Tolkien soon found that the classics course he had chosen, covered the whole range of classical study: Latin and Greek authors such as Aeschylus, Homer, Cicero and Virgil, as well as classical philosophy and history such as in Plato, Tacitus and others. He lost much of his joy in the ancient writers under the rigorous syllabus, and in later years confessed: 'My love for the classics took ten years to recover from lectures on Cicero and Demosthenes.' The situation was not helped by the absence of a resident classical tutor in Exeter College for the first two terms of his time there.

While at school Tolkien had discovered philology, the historic study of language and culture; he was thus saved from disaster at college by being allowed to choose a special subject, his choice being comparative philology. This meant that the pre-eminent philologist Joseph Wright began tutoring Tolkien at Exeter College; this being the same Wright who had written the *Primer of the Gothic Language* that Tolkien had obtained while a schoolboy and had so enjoyed. Joseph Wright had started out as a Yorkshire wool-mill worker when he was only six years old and taught himself to read at the age of 15; through a long struggle he became Professor of Comparative Philology at Oxford. Among the many languages he later studied were Sanskrit, Gothic, Russian, Old Norse,

and Old and Middle High German; Wright was to significantly inspire Tolkien in his future work.

Tolkien did well in comparative philology and as a result of his success, he was able to switch from studying the classics to studying English language and literature, with a focus on early English. Significantly, this meant the difference between achieving a poor degree, which would have ruled out an academic career, and gaining a First Class one.

THE ORIGINAL TWERP?

Thomas Wade Earp was a fellow undergraduate and acquaintance of Tolkien's at Exeter College, who went on to write about modern painters. He was one of the editors of the publication Oxford Poetry 1915, *which included Tolkien's first published poem* Goblin Feet. *His initials and surname – T. W. Earp – is likely to have given rise to the expression 'twerp', which originated in the English language around 1910. Furthermore, in a letter written many years later, Tolkien refers to Earp as 'the original twerp'.*

J.R.R. TOLKIEN'S FELLOWSHIP OF FRIENDS

The T.C.B.S.
A fellowship of tea and cakes

As a boy, J.R.R. Tolkien attended King Edward VI Grammar School in the centre of Birmingham; it was here that he formed a club with a number of friends. Three of them became particularly close to him: G.B. Smith, R.Q. 'Rob' Gilson and Christopher Wiseman. Poignantly, from his group of close friends only Wiseman was to survive the First World War.

At first, the group called themselves the Tea Club (T.C.) as they met in the school library where they made cups of tea and snacked on cakes. They subsequently changed their name to the Barrovian Society (B.S.) in honour of the tearoom in Barrow's Stores on nearby Corporation Street that became a favourite meeting place.

Gilson was the son of the head teacher at King Edward's; Smith

Aerial view of the Somme Battlefield

was a gifted poet whose verses were published as a book after the war; and Wiseman shared many of Tolkien's interests, his challenging comments on Tolkien's early writings playing an important role as critique for the author. He also persuaded Tolkien to edit Smith's poems for publication.

Sadly, Geoffrey Bache Smith was killed on active service in the winter of 1916, aged just 22 years. He wrote to Tolkien shortly before his death, speaking of how the T.C.B.S. – the 'immortal four' – would live on, even if he died that night. Smith concluded: 'May God bless you, my dear John Ronald, and may you say the things I have tried to say long after I am not there to say them, if such be my lot.'

Although Tolkien and Wiseman met infrequently after the war, their friendship was never entirely forgotten. The T.C.B.S. left a permanent mark on Tolkien, which he captured in the idea of a 'fellowship' in *The Fellowship of the Ring*, part of his most famous story, *The Lord of the Rings*. His later close friendship with C. S. Lewis, and their Oxford group of literary friends known as the Inklings, helped to satisfy this important side of his personality.

WAR CASUALTIES
Two of Tolkien's three close friends in the T.C.B.S., like him, saw action in the Battle of the Somme in 1916, one of the bloodiest in the First World War. 'Rob' Gilson died on the first day of the battle, and G.B.

Smith shortly after the battle was over. Others friends from Tolkien's schooldays also died during the war. Tolkien's brother, Hilary, survived it despite being wounded on occasions. Tolkien could also be said to have been a casualty of war, since his experiences during that period were to traumatize him.

Council of London
War focuses the minds of friends

At the onset of the First World War, J.R.R. Tolkien's close school friends, known as the T.C.B.S., were now at university and had to decide how to respond to the call up. The war had the effect of focussing the purpose of the T.C.B.S., at least on some members. It had passed beyond its initial existence as a school club into something that might clarify what university study, poetry writing, art and architecture were all about.

One of the group's members, Christopher Wiseman, was studying at Cambridge. He thought a great deal about the possible function of the T.C.B.S. going forwards,

not only in its members' lives but also in wider society and culture; he thus had the idea of calling a 'Council of London'. His parents had recently moved to the city, and his new home was large enough to accommodate those he considered should be core members: Tolkien, Smith and Gilson were duly invited.

The four met in the Christmas vacation of 1914, purging the club of the other members to purify its aim. The Council was to have a far-reaching effect on the direction of Tolkien's thinking and imagination; in fact, it changed all four members

Christmas card from Tolkien's childhood (1892)

in various ways. In the absence of the others, they were able to focus on issues fundamental to them, such as Christian faith, human love, patriotism, and a nation's right of self-rule, which were the forces that they felt moved them. Moreover, they felt they shared a potent vision that could shake the world, which Tolkien saw as reigniting an old light.

Their contribution would centre on their individual gifts: Gilson's inclined to architecture and art; Smith's was in poetry; Wiseman's were not so clear, being multi-gifted and inclined to science as well as art. For Tolkien, the Council of London opened a door, providing him with a 'voice for all kind of pent up things'. It was at the Council that he decided he was a poet; later, he saw that London weekend marked a change of direction and a renewal of vision. This inspiration and determination was deepened by the loss of Gilson and Smith in the war, and his own survival of the trenches of the Somme.

Exeter College Essay Club
A sounding board for the young author

In October 1911, J.R.R. Tolkien entered Exeter College in Oxford and an under-graduate school named *Literae Humaniores*, which was dominated by the classics. He was soon to avail himself of various undergraduate clubs, including the college Essay Club.

Francis Thompson

After switching to the Oxford Honours English school, Tolkien presented to the club a paper on Norse sagas, as a result of his exploration deeper and deeper into the world of northern mythology. He also read to the club an essay on the verse of the Roman Catholic Francis Thompson, from whom he received inspiration in his own quest to be a poet. Moreover, on 27 November 1914, he presented his poem *The Voyage of Eärendel* to the Essay Club, thereby exposing to fellow undergraduates the very beginning of his unfolding creation, Middle-earth. Ironically, on that occasion few attended as the student population, eagerly volunteering for service, was thinning due to the outbreak of the First World War.

After serving in the British army, Tolkien returned to Oxford to work on the *Oxford English Dictionary* and to tutor. At that time, he revisited the freshly re-formed Essay Club at his old college. This time he read 'The Fall of Gondolin' from his burgeoning tales of Middle-earth; among the undergraduates of Exeter College on that occasion were Hugo Dyson

and Nevill Coghill. In later years, they would become members of the Inklings, the literary club that Tolkien would also attend; they were therefore the first of that future circle of friends to hear any of his invented mythology. 'The Fall of Gondolin' in a revised form would eventually be published posthumously in *The Silmarillion*, nearly 60 years after that initial reading to the Essay Club.

The Inklings
A rich diversity of Oxford friends

The Inklings were an informal group of Oxford friends who met to read out from their writings, or just to talk. As the Inklings existed in varying shapes over nearly three decades, and as there was no formal membership or minute-taking at its meetings, the group is hard to label. To gain a view of it, we must rely on scattered details written in letters by members, tantalizing details in the engaging diaries of C.S. Lewis's brother, Major Warren Lewis, memories captured in memoirs, and other similar sources.

Unlike most of the societies and

The Eagle and Child in St Giles, Oxford

groups to which J.R.R. Tolkien belonged during his more than 30 years as an Oxford Professor, the Inklings were not made up entirely of dons. They included men from several professions, including a G.P., a retired Army Major, and a lawyer; even the Oxford dons themselves represented several academic disciplines, not English language and literature alone. At the centre of the Inklings was Tolkien's close friend, C.S. Lewis. In fact, the Inklings developed from Lewis's circle of friends, and were usually devout Christians, at least in the earlier years, with a diversity of views. Tolkien once described the 'club' as being 'like-minded'.

The Inklings began around 1933,

when an undergraduate society of the same name, which Tolkien and C.S. Lewis had attended by invitation, closed. The name was transferred to the circle of friends with whom Lewis habitually met, including his newly retired brother, Warren Lewis, H.V.D. 'Hugo' Dyson, Nevill Coghill, Owen Barfield, and Tolkien. In early years, the Inklings also included Lewis's G.P. Dr 'Humphrey' Havard, the scholar Charles Wrenn, and the theologian Adam Fox. The Inklings was still a small group at the start of its golden age, the years of the Second World War and immediately after. Later, the friends were joined by the remarkable figure Charles Williams, an editor with the Oxford University

Press, and an author. He was with the Inklings from the onset of war in 1939 until his sudden death in 1945, just following V.E. day. After the war, the numbers of attendees increased significantly.

For much of their existence, the Inklings were focused upon being a reading group, often meeting in Lewis's rooms at Magdalen College, despite there being members who wrote little; the friends also met more informally to chat in favourite pubs, including The Eagle and Child in St Giles', Oxford. After 1949, the Inklings' reading group appears to have ceased, thus coinciding with Tolkien's completion of *The Lord of the Rings*. He had read much of this, and also *The Hobbit,* to his group of friends, and such readings became an important part of his creative process.

'Tollers' and 'Jack'
Tolkien's friendship with Lewis

J.R.R. Tolkien and C.S. Lewis may have made an odd duo, but they contributed profoundly to each other's work: certainly, without their friendship we would be bereft of either *The Lord of the Rings* or *The Chronicles of Narnia*. Tolkien was to acknowledge that, but for the encouragement of his friend, he never would have completed the writing of *The Lord of the Rings*. As for C.S. Lewis, he owed it in large part to Tolkien for helping him in the final stage of his long pilgrimage from atheism to Christian belief. It was this belief that became the vision behind the Narnia stories, in particular giving the spirited, magnificent lion Aslan who created the magical world in which the tales are set.

Tolkien and Lewis first encountered each other at a meeting of the Oxford University English School faculty at Merton College on 11 March 1926. Lewis had been a tutor and lecturer in English for nearly one academic year; Tolkien, the older of the two, had for the same period held the Chair of Anglo-Saxon. 'No harm in him: only needs a smack or so,' wrote C.S. Lewis, or 'Jack' to his friends, in his diary on the day he first met Tolkien, nicknamed 'Tollers' at times. The latter was, at least in Lewis's view, rather opinionated, hence the need for a 'smack or so'.

Some of Tolkien's strongest opinions arose from his Roman Catholicism; at that time Lewis was something of a doubting atheist, but still committed to a materialistic explanation of life and of the origins of human language. However, Tolkien soon noticed that there were chinks in his new friend's armour, and any initial antipathy was quickly forgotten. The two, who soon became fast friends, differed in temperament, approach to faith, and views of their art. Nevertheless, their deep affinities brought them together for almost 40 years of friendship.

The spell of other worlds

Tolkien showed Lewis his beautiful prose translation of *Beowulf* and shared drafts detailing his largely private world of Middle-earth. Lewis's response was more than Tolkien could have hoped for: the young sceptic was enraptured. He had always been captivated by ancient myths and stories of 'romance' – that is, tales that contained glimpses of other worlds – yet here were tales by a modern-day author, as elaborate and compelling as

any he had read.

Soon Tolkien began trying to convince his friend of the truth of Christian faith, arguing that the Gospels of Christ have a satisfying imaginative as well as intellectual appeal, which demanded a response from the whole person. He accused Lewis of imaginative failure in not accepting their reality; only a few days later Lewis was to capitulate to these arguments, and become a Christian believer.

Statue of C. S. Lewis, East Belfast

Fantasy and fairy tales, at the time of Tolkien and Lewis's first meeting, were still considered literature suitable for children only. It was Tolkien who effectively enlisted Lewis in the task of rehabilitating these kinds of stories, once enjoyed by warriors in the mead halls, and robust enough to become a vehicle for exploring the complexity of modern questions such as global warfare and human evil on an unprecedented scale.

ULSTERIOR MOTIVE

Among Tolkien's unpublished papers are comments late in life upon his friend, C.S. Lewis, called 'The Ulsterior Motive'. Over the years the friends disagreed theologically, discussing many affinities and differences: Tolkien was a traditional Roman Catholic – whom Lewis insensitively at times would label a 'Papist' – and Lewis had returned to an orthodox Anglican faith. Lewis had grown up in the north of Ireland at a time when the discontents that led to the eventual partition were rife. In his paper Tolkien, in a rather jaundiced way, suggested that his friend was reverting to
his Ulster Protestant background. In fact, Lewis's quest for common ground in his advocacy of 'mere Christianity' would be anathema to hard liners on both sides of the Protestant–Catholic divide.

Charles Williams
An enigmatic friend

Charles Williams was a charismatic poet, a writer of supernatural thrillers, a biographer, a theological thinker and a literary critic, who was introduced to J.R.R. Tolkien and the literary circle of the Inklings in the 1930s, after C.S. Lewis made contact with him in 1936. When Williams was transferred to Oxford from London at the beginning of the Second World War, he became a member of the group and Tolkien saw him frequently at its meetings and on other occasions. Tolkien found it difficult to understand many of his writings, particularly his poetry, because of their obscurity; of the Inklings, only C.S. Lewis was truly on his wavelength.

Born in Islington, London, Williams gained a place at University College in its city, beginning his studies at the age of 15. His family ran out of funds for his fees and he was unable to complete his course; nevertheless, Williams eventually joined the Oxford University Press' London office, first as a proofreader. He married and began holding adult evening classes in literature on behalf of London County Council to supplement his modest income; he wrote a series of seven supernatural thrillers, including *The Place of the Lion* (1931), for the same reason.

When Williams was evacuated with the O.U.P. to Oxford, he, in John Wain's words, 'gave himself as unreservedly to Oxford as Oxford gave itself to him'; Oxford University recognized Charles Williams in 1943 with an honorary M.A. After his unexpected death, several of the Inklings – including Tolkien, C.S. Lewis, Owen Barfield, and Warren Lewis – contributed to a posthumous tribute, *Essays Presented to Charles Williams* (1945). Tolkien appreciated his friend's comments regarding the unfinished *The Lord of the Rings*, particularly after Williams borrowed from him the typescript of what had been written so far.

The poet T.S. Eliot, his publisher and a great admirer of Williams' writings, said: 'For him there was no frontier between the material and the spiritual world. Had I ever to spend a night in a haunted house, I should have felt secure with Williams in my company; he was somehow protected from evil, and was himself a protection…The deeper things are there just because they belonged to

T.S. Eliot

the world he lived in, and he could not have kept them out.'

THE LEWIS SÉANCE

Tolkien became unhappy with Charles Williams' influence over C.S. Lewis and his distinctive presence in the Inklings meetings; he came to feel that it weakened his ties of friendship with Lewis. Furthermore, Tolkien was particularly uneasy about the occult elements in Williams' thrillers and late in life, he referred back to Williams rather tetchily as a 'witch-doctor'. In earlier years, Tolkien had appreciated Williams' insight into the supernatural, writing in an affectionate poem to him: 'When Charles is on his trail the devil squeals, / for cloven feet have vulnerable heels.' However in a letter dated June 1944, he referred to the meetings of the Inklings as the 'Lewis séance'.

THE TOLKIEN PHENOMENON

The Times obituary
Written by Lewis who died ten years earlier

J.R.R. Tolkien died on 2 September 1973, taken ill while visiting friends in Bournemouth. The next day, *The Times* published a polished and very informative account of his life in an obituary. Tolkien's friend and Oxford colleague, C.S. Lewis, had died nearly ten years earlier, in November 1963. Yet Tolkien's official biographer, Humphrey Carpenter, revealed that the author of the obituary was Lewis, a fact that other scholars now accept. Furthermore Edith, Tolkien's wife, had previously told the US scholar Clyde S. Kilby that Lewis was writing her husband's obituary. Indeed, *The Times* piece seems to have been written quite some time before Lewis's death, although a reference to Tolkien's award of Commander of the British Empire

(C.B.E) in 1972 had been added.

In fact, the obituary is one of the best brief biographies of Tolkien, full of important insights; another is that of Tom Shippey in the *Oxford Dictionary of National Biography*. The *Times* obituary tells us, for instance, that Tolkien 'had been inside language. He had not gone far…with his invention before he discovered that every language presupposes a mythology; and at once began to fill in the mythology presupposed by Elvish.' We are informed also, in those days before the flood of posthumous publications, that: 'Only a tithe of the poems, translations, articles, lectures and notes in which his multifarious interest found expression ever reached the printer.'

The Lord of the Rings critiqued
From 'juvenile trash' to 'lightning from a clear sky'

As a work of literature, the merits and demerits of *The Lord of the Rings* have been critiqued by countless scholars and readers; to this day it continues to divide the

W.H. Auden

critics. Among its admirers is the distinguished poet W.H. Auden. In his *New York Times* review of *The Return of the King* on 22 January 1956 he reflects: 'I rarely remember a book about which I have had such violent arguments. Nobody *seems* to have a moderate opinion: either, like myself, people find it a masterpiece of its genre or they cannot abide it, and among the hostile there are some, I must confess, for whose literary judgment I have great respect.' Also lavish with his praise is Tolkien's friend and Oxford colleague C.S. Lewis, who opens his review of *The Fellowship of the Ring* thus: 'This book is like lightning from a clear sky'; later he adds 'here are beauties which pierce like swords or burn like cold iron'.

Other literary critics of the time such as Edmund Wilson and Philip Toynbee disdain *The Lord of the Rings*. In 1956 Wilson dismisses the first volume, *The Fellowship of the Ring*, as juvenile, pre-teenage trash – not, interestingly, adult trash. In 1961, Toynbee looks back and concludes that Tolkien's books are 'dull, ill-written, whimsical and childish [and they] have passed into a merciful oblivion'. Furthermore, the critic Jared Lobdell comments that, at the time, 'no "mainstream critic" appreciated *The Lord of the Rings* or indeed was in a position to write criticism on it—most being unsure what it was and why readers liked it'.

Critics have remained divided over the decades since the publication of the book in the mid-1950s. Yet, on trial alongside *The Lord of the Rings* is the whole genre of fantasy, so much of which was allowed to blossom through Tolkien's pioneering work in creating modern fantasy for an adult readership. Professor Tom Shippey goes so far as to suggest: 'The dominant literary mode of the twentieth century has been the fantastic.' He cites writers of fantasy and other symbolic literature such as parable and science fiction including George Orwell, William Golding, Kurt Vonnegut, Ursula LeGuin and Thomas Pynchon. If Shippey is correct, adequately describing Tolkien's work and achievement is at the very heart of appreciating both what mainstream literature is, and its wider reception by readers.

What's in a name?
How The Hobbit *got published*

J.R.R. Tolkien often told of how *The Hobbit*, his classic story for children set in the Third Age of Middle-Earth, began its life. One summer, he says, he was marking school exam scripts when he came across a blank page. Happy for a pause in his relentless task, he scribbled across it: 'In a hole in the ground there lived a hobbit.' At first glance, this does not appear to tell us much about how the book started as that sentence is what became the first line. Yet Tolkien's account is truly revealing as names had often suggested stories to him; he had no idea what a Hobbit was, so he had to find out.

The result of Tolkien discovering what Hobbits are is the book we know as *The Hobbit*. That initial scrawled sentence grew into a story that Tolkien told his children, which he eventually wrote down. The tale developed further as its hero, Mr Bilbo Baggins, left the untroubled comfort of The Shire with a company of dwarves and a wizard to encounter strange creatures and places in the wider world. Furthermore, the story was gradually to attach itself to the world of Middle-earth, with its long history that Tolkien had been capturing in poems, stories and other material since he was a young man. The introduction of Hobbits to Tolkien's imagined world was dramatically to affect the course of events there.

Travels of a typescript

By the beginning of 1933, Tolkien was able to hand to his close friend C.S. Lewis a sheaf of papers to read. Comprising a largely typed-up draft, scholars are divided on whether the story was then reasonably complete. Christopher Tolkien points out that, initially, chapters towards the end of it were rough and presented in handwriting. Lewis, who was familiar with much of what Tolkien had already written about Middle-earth, loved this new story about Hobbits.

Tolkien also lent an unfinished copy of *The Hobbit* to a former student. Through her, it came to the notice of a publisher, George Allen and Unwin, when one of their staff, Susan Dagnal, visited Oxford. Dagnal read *The Hobbit* and became convinced it should be published. When Tolkien eventually sent in the final typescript to the publisher, Stanley Unwin, then head of publishing, gave it to his ten-year-old son Raynor to read. The boy earned a fee of one shilling for his report, which was positive.

FEATURED IN DICTIONARIES

*The word 'hobbit' has become accepted into the English language and is now featured in larger dictionaries, such as the **Oxford English Dictionary**. The **O.E.D.** acknowledges J.R.R. Tolkien as the creator of the word's usual meaning. However, it also lists two old local usages for 'hobbit' or 'hobbet', meaning either a seed-basket that is also called a 'hoppet', or a measure equivalent to two-and-a-half bushels. Tolkien was apparently unaware of this latter, rare usage.*

Two-and-a-half bushels

Hobbit-forming
An explosion of interest

When *The Lord of the Rings* was published in the mid-1950s, J.R.R. Tolkien's publishers were expecting it to lose them money. However, soon the three hardback volumes were making a quiet but substantial income in both the UK and Commonwealth, and also in the USA. Appreciative letters began to arrive, including one from a Mr Sam Gamgee of Tooting, London in March 1956; Tolkien was relieved not to receive one from a Mr S. Gollum. The book and its author continued to be featured in the media after the initial reviews and, in 1957, BBC Radio broadcast a dramatized version of the book; there was also talk of a movie version.

However, this all changed in the mid-1960s when a loophole in US Copyright Law at the time helped make *The Lord of the Rings* an international cultural phenomenon. Ace Books published an unauthorized paperback edition, for which the author would receive not a penny. A Tolkien fan society began to support

The Beatles

the campaign of Tolkien and his official publishers against Ace Books. The resulting publicity helped that fan society to grow enormously, and started to bring Tolkien's name into mainstream youth culture in the USA and then across the globe.

Amazingly, the world of Hobbits, wizards and The Shire was soon helping to express a hippie culture; slogans like 'Gandalf for President' and 'Frodo Lives' were everywhere. One of the most vibrant expressions of this culture was via rock music, with bands such as Led Zeppelin referring to Tolkien's stories in their compositions. The Beatles even planned to make a movie of *The Lord of the Rings* with the band playing the lead roles. Furthermore, in 1969 one famous slogan, 'Tolkien is hobbit-

forming', was spotted on a wall in Balliol College, Oxford.

In the various cultural shifts of the following decades, Tolkien's fan base continued to grow and to diversify, its global reach increasing. As the end of the millennium approached, it became clear that Tolkien's readership and impact upon popular culture made a high-budget movie possible. Moreover, the new medium of computer graphics made possible a viable imaginative representation of the story. The New Zealand filmmaker Peter Jackson had a convincing setting for Middle-earth to hand in the backdrop of his native country, and the determination to overcome all obstacles. His movie trilogy was to create a significant cultural storm in the first few years of the new millennium.

RINGERS: LORD OF THE FANS

Ringers: Lord of the Fans *(2005)* is a feature length, fun documentary, which sprang from one of the leading Tolkien fan websites, The One Ring Net (TORN). Ringers describes the diversity of J.R.R.

Leonard Nimroy

*Tolkien's fans and the cultural shifts through which this fandom has travelled; it also catalogues the impact of Tolkien on popular culture right into the era of the internet. The clip of the actor Leonard Nimoy of **Star Trek** fame singing his ridiculously enjoyable 'Bilbo Baggins' song that is featured in the documentary emphasizes the fact that it retains a firm and valuable perspective on what is really a very complex phenomenon.*

From publishing risk to bestseller
How The Lord of the Rings *got published*

The idea of writing a sequel to J.R.R. Tolkien's popular children's story *The Hobbit* came from his publisher, Stanley (later Sir Stanley) Unwin of George Allen and Unwin. As one of several outstanding independent publishing houses in those early post-war years, the company naturally wished to follow the commercial success of *The Hobbit* with a sequel to secure further profits.

Although the new story gradually shifted from being aimed at children to becoming one aimed at an adult readership, Unwin persisted in encouraging his author. Tolkien completed writing *The Lord of the Rings* in a reasonably complete draft by 1949, almost 12 years after starting work on it. Even so, the first two volumes – *The Fellowship of the Ring* and *The Two Towers* – would not be published until a further five years later, in 1954, with *The Return of the King* appearing the following year, in 1955.

One reason for the long delay between completion and publication was Tolkien's understandable perfectionism; he constantly tinkered with and augmented the complex text, including the addition of a raft of appendices. Another reason for the delay was that Tolkien wished to finish writing and publish *The Silmarillion* with *The Lord of the Rings*, as the former explained the history of Middle-earth prior to the events of Frodo's quest in the latter. Despite the usual support of his publisher, Stanley Unwin quite reasonably declined publishing *The Silmarillion*. Undeterred, Tolkien sent the typescripts of both titles to an interested editor at another publisher, William Collins, supposing from the editor's initial response that there was a good chance both would be published. When Tolkien eventually realized that this was not to be the case, he returned repentantly to Unwin with just *The Lord of the Rings*.

Negative risk assessment

Stanley Unwin remained enthusiastic and sent his son Raynor to Oxford to pick up the original, and only, manuscript of *The Lord of the Rings*. Because of its length, father and son decided to publish the work as hardback in three parts. When the production costs were calculated, it became clear in the light of standard expectations that *The Lord of the Rings* would make a loss. Nevertheless, both Stanley Unwin and his son were still keen to continue with its publication. As a result, Tolkien signed a contract with George Allen and Unwin for the book that specified a share in any profits, rather than the usual percentage royalty on sales.

It turned out that Tolkien was to earn vastly more than if he had received the usual royalty payments. The first printing in the UK of *The Fellowship of the Ring* was just 3,000 copies. But then a US publisher came on board, reprints of the three volumes became unexpectedly frequent, and profits steadily rose. Up until 2007, the estimated sales of *The Lord of the Rings* in all languages were around 150 million copies (counting three-volume editions as one unit).

J.R.R. Tolkien in the media
The work of 'other minds and hands'

In creating his stories and other material about Middle-earth, including *The Lord of the Rings*, J.R.R. Tolkien had a vision of creating a vast mythology that he could dedicate to his country. He saw there were other mythologies, such as Celtic, Greek, Finnish and Scandinavian, and he was trying to fill in what he felt was lacking – a mythology for England. His mythology, he decided, would possess a quality evocative of Britain and northwest Europe. Tolkien's hope, he once wrote, had been to render some of his stories in detail and leave others merely sketched. Thereby, each part would suggest a greater whole, yet leave room for the creativity of others employing drama, music and painting to fulfil this. He later concluded that his hope had been empty.

However, since the publication of *The Lord of the Rings* between 1954 and 1955, there have been many adaptations of the work by others in movie, radio, theatre, music and other arts, suggesting that Tolkien's hope and vision was not meaningless. No doubt, Tolkien typically would have disapproved of a good number of these adaptations, but the fact remains that many are in keeping with his vision of 'other minds and hands' freely and creatively filling in dimensions of his Middle-earh mythology. Here, one could consider of the music of Stephen Oliver, Donald Swann or Howard Shore as their work interpreted his stories and verse.

There have been two movie adaptations of *The Lord of the Rings*. The first was the incomplete *The Lord of the Rings* (1978): animator Ralph Bakshi adapted *The Fellowship of the Ring* and *The Two Towers* as one movie, but was unable to finance his intended second movie on the remainder of the story; instead, he compromised with a television animation as the vehicle for this. The second movie adaptation was Peter Jackson's trilogy: *The Fellowship of the Ring* (2001), *The Two Towers* (2002) and *The Return of the King* (2003). Jackson commented to his biographer,

Brian Sibley: 'The moment you think of fantasy, you think of Tolkien.' Indeed, Jackson was able to leap over all the hurdles to create a masterpiece of cinema and has since returned once again to adapting Tolkien in movie form, with his two-part version of *The Hobbit* due for re lease in 2012 and 2013, retold as an adult story.

Several audio book adaptations of *The Lord of the Rings* have appeared over the years, including Rob Inglis' version. An audacious musical version appeared first in Toronto in 2006 for six months, and then moved to London's West End in 2007, there repeating its lack of success; there have been other stage versions of *The Lord of the Rings* in the USA. *The Hobbit* has been adapted at times for the stage, often in school productions. As an Oxford undergraduate, the British writer, Humphrey Carpenter, adapted one such production for New College School; performed by 11- to

13-year-old boys, Tolkien himself attended the final performance. Carpenter recalled that while Tolkien enjoyed some of the play, he did not approve of the 'tinkering with the story' that had taken place. A graphic novel of *The Hobbit* was published in 1989-90, adapted by Charles Dixon and illustrated by David Wenzel.

B.B.C. ADAPTATIONS

The British Broadcasting Corporation (B.B.C.) has adapted Tolkien's work for radio. In December 1953, a dramatization of his modern translation of **Sir Gawain** *and the* **Green Knight** *was broadcast, with an introduction to the Middle English poem. Then in 1955 and 1956, a 12-part radio adaptation of* **The Lord of the Rings** *was aired. In 1981, a new dramatization was broadcast in 26 half-hour instalments, adapted largely by Brian Sibley. A version of it made available on audiotape and later CD has become popular ever since.*

J.R.R. TOLKIEN'S FAITH

A spiritual home
The Birmingham Oratory and Cardinal Newman

Four years after being widowed J.R.R. Tolkien's mother, Mabel, converted to Roman Catholicism; it was to his mother that Tolkien owed his own entry into Catholicism as a child. Searching for a spiritual home for herself and her two boys, she came across the Birmingham Oratory in Edgbaston, and eventually moved the family close by. Attached to it was the Oratory School, which later relocated to Berkshire where it remains as an independent, Roman Catholic boarding school for boys.

The influential Cardinal Henry Newman had founded the community of the Birmingham Oratory in 1849. The Cardinal also set up an Oratory in London and wished to set up a similar institution in Oxford, although an Oratory was not established until 1993, located at the church of St Aloysius, where Tolkien regularly worshipped during his early years as an Oxford Professor.

At the Birmingham Oratory, Mabel met a kindly priest named Father Francis Morgan, who had served under Newman and was well versed in the Cardinal's approach to faith, life and education. He took the family under his wing and, after Mabel's death, became guardian to Tolkien as well as to his brother,

The Birmingham Oratory

- 114 -

Hilary, following her wishes. He took the orphans on holiday to Lyme Regis and elsewhere, found them accommodation, and cared for them in many other ways, including financially. The boys became a familiar part of the Oratory community.

THE ORATORY SCHOOL

Tolkien had a warm association with the Oratory School near Reading through his son Michael, who taught there for a while. Indeed, part of **The Lord of the Rings** *was written at the school as the book neared completion, Tolkien staying in a master's room and working on his manuscript for much of the long summer vacation of 1949.*

Tolkien's Roman Catholic faith
How it influenced The Lord of the Rings

J.R.R. Tolkien saw himself light-heartedly as a Hobbit, and more seriously as a Christian. His Roman Catholic faith was orthodox, which gave him immense common ground with those whose denominations were other than Roman Catholic, such as his friend and colleague, C.S. Lewis. With such believers, he shared a 'catholic' faith, even though it was not Roman Catholic.

In a letter, he stated his view that *The Lord of the Rings* was a 'fundamentally religious and Catholic work; unconsciously so at first, but consciously in the revision'; that is, it was endued with his religious insights. Moreover, he was delighted when a fellow Roman Catholic named Father Robert Murray wrote to him that what he had read of the book had 'a positive compatibility with the order of Grace', likening the beauty of Galadriel to the Virgin Mary. Tolkien regarded any such religious elements as being 'absorbed into' the story rather than being explicit. He felt that openly religious references would mar the impact and consistency of the story upon the reader.

His devout Christian faith and commitment to Catholicism went back to his childhood and the influence of his mother, who passed away at the age of 34 when he was only 12. As a Catholic, he was conservative, preferring to hear the liturgy in Latin and making confession before taking the Mass. As a schoolboy, one of his closest friends was a Methodist. Although at times, he felt C.S. Lewis was regressing towards Ulster Protestantism, and disagreed with him over re-marriage, cremation of the body and popularizing theology, the pair remained friends for nearly 40 years, and very close friends for a great deal of that time. There is no doubt that Tolkien sought friends who shared his faith, even if they did not share his churchmanship.

The clearest expression of his views

on how religious and Christian faith relates to stories of the kind he liked to read and write is in his published essay 'On fairy-stories', which expands his Andrew Lang lecture at the University of St Andrews in 1939.

Eucatastrophe
The sudden, happy turn in a story

We speak of 'the darkness before dawn' to express harrowing experiences that are followed by something good, yet Tolkien explored an idea which touched human hopes and fears even deeper. In this idea, there is crisis and apparent catastrophe with no sense of a happy outcome; then occurs a sudden, unexpected turn of events that is shockingly good. This is why he wrote of the consolation of this kind of happy ending, coining the term 'eucatastrophe' to describe it.

He argued that the term, which might translate as a 'good' catastrophe, is the highest achievement of a fairy tale, his definition for a story that creates another world where Elves and similar magical creatures exist. That other world might be on the borders of the story, or at the very heart of it. Although people usually invent such stories, it is possible for events to take place in actual history that have all the qualities of a fairy tale or myth, including a eucatastrophe.

Tolkien's word has now been added to the *Oxford English Dictionary,* which defines a eucatastrophe as follows: 'Especially in a fictional narrative: a (sudden or unexpected) favourable turn of events; *especially* a resolution of this type; a happy ending.' The *Dictionary* also quotes from a letter Tolkien's own definition, as follows: 'the sudden happy turn in a story which pierces you with a joy that brings tears'.

In his essay 'On fairy-stories', Tolkien explicitly links the consolation offered by the eucatastrophe with the Christian gospel, where there occurs in its first-century history two events he identifies as eucatastrophic. In his words: 'The Birth of Christ is the eucatastrophe of Man's history. The Resurrection is the eucatastrophe of the story of the Incarnation.' Thus, human history tells a story in which

the Creator of all appears, taking on human flesh at the Incarnation, which is the first sudden turn in the story. The later, otherwise tragic story of Christ's violent death also has a sudden, unexpected turn in the form of his return to physical life.

When Tolkien recognized the reality and importance of the sudden, happy turn – the eucatastrophe – he realized that he had already been seeking to feature it in his fiction. The recognition brought together the heart of his imaginative creations and his Christian beliefs as both, as he saw it, pointed to a single truth.

The Virgin Mary
Her impact upon J.R.R. Tolkien

J.R.R. Tolkien was a devout Christian who adhered to the authority of the Roman Catholic Church. He held a high view of Mary, the mother of Jesus, which incorporated the particular decrees of his Church such as that of the Immaculate Conception. His faith and devotion to Mary was linked with that of his own mother who had been ostracized by her family,

The Madonna in Sorrow, *by Sassoferrato*

some understanding of the depths of veneration for Mary held by Roman Catholics in general, and Tolkien in particular. In a letter, Tolkien admitted that there was much of Christian and Roman Catholic thinking and imagining about Mary behind his portrayal of Galadriel's character. However, there were also important differences; he pointed out that Galadriel had to repent for wrongdoing in her ancient past, where she was implicated in a rebellion by a group of Elves against the Valar, the angelic powers.

when a widow with two young sons, for joining the Roman Catholic Church; indeed, he believed that this was a contributing factor to her early death. Furthermore, Tolkien was pleased when W.H. Auden confided to him that his title poem, in his book *Homage to Clio* (1960), was a 'hymn to Our Lady'.

The devotion of Sam Gamgee the Hobbit and Gimli the dwarf to Galadriel the Elven princess in *The Lord of the Rings* provides

God in fiction
Remaining in step with his beliefs

In J.R.R. Tolkien's *The Silmarillion* the name of the God figure, his creator of the world, is Ilúvatar, which means 'Father of All'; he is also called Eru, which means 'the One'. At the beginning of the book, the 'Ainulindalë' records how, when creating the angelic powers, Ilúvatar revealed to them the themes of creation in music; as his agents, they subsequently helped to realize his vision by making the world.

Although, on the face of it, God seems absent from the events of Middle-earth, in fact its very history is the outworking of the themes of the music played at the beginning of creation. Consequently, the providence and grace of Ilúvatar is a constant reality throughout the tales of Middle-earth. The will of Ilúvatar in shaping the events of Middle-earth emphasizes Tolkien's idea of 'sub-creation', his term for the creation of secondary worlds.

In reading his fiction, one is aware of the mind and will of the maker and teller of the tale: Tolkien. He believed that through making and telling stories we exercise a God-given right to be a sub-creator. If done with skill, our creation evokes the actual, primary world. The human creator as imitator parallels the divine creator, although in a limited way, as God does not imitate but originates as the author of all.

In Tolkien's mythology, Elves and humankind are called 'The Children of Ilúvatar' as they are the special and direct creations of God, not the handiwork of the angelic powers who assist him in creation. Their fate has an element of mystery to it: the immortal Elves are to be forever tied up with the world, whereas the destiny of 'mortal man doomed to die' is to be greater.

These sort of theological and philosophical themes constantly preoccupied Tolkien as he built his mythology over the years. His desire to remain in harmony with his bedrock beliefs, while following his invention wherever it led him, contributed to his difficulty and eventual inability to complete his work on his body of mythology, *The Silmarillion*.

Churches associated with J.R.R. Tolkien
A regular and conscientious worshipper

Apart for some lapses in his devotions while a student at Oxford, J.R.R. Tolkien conscientiously took confession, Mass and practised other duties of his Roman Catholic faith throughout his life. Consequently, he became associated with a number of churches or institutions of faith over the years.

St Aloysius's Roman Catholic Church, Oxford

Most formative on Tolkien was undoubtedly the Birmingham Oratory in Edgbaston. His mother, Mabel, had converted to the Roman Catholic faith as a young widow and single parent; she took him here, along with his younger brother, after failing to find a local Catholic church at which she felt at home. The Oratory provided protection and pastoral support to the family and, after Mabel's untimely death, one of its priests became the guardian of Tolkien and his brother.

Another church associated with Tolkien was the Church of St Mary the Immaculate in Warwick. Here Tolkien and Edith Bratt married on Wednesday 22 March 1916, not long before he left for the war in France. There he saw action in the Battle of the Somme where he was wounded;

he subsequently returned to England to recuperate. During the many moves of this recuperation period, a church he and Edith often attended was St John the Baptist Roman Catholic Church in Great Haywood.

After the war, Tolkien returned to Oxford, bringing with him Edith and baby John, together with Edith's cousin, Jennie Grove. It may have been then that he started attending St Aloysius's Roman Catholic Church on the Woodstock Road, a short walk away. When the family returned again to Oxford early in 1926 after Tolkien's spell teaching in Leeds, he again worshipped at St Aloysius's. At this point the church was some distance from where they then lived in Northmoor Road, and Tolkien occasionally worshipped elsewhere, a favourite church being St Gregory and St Augustine Roman Catholic Church in Upper Wolvercote. Over a quarter of a century later, when Tolkien and his wife moved to 76 Sandfield Road in the Oxford suburb of Headington, Tolkien attended St Anthony's Church on Headley Way.

J.R.R. TOLKIEN'S INSPIRATIONS

J.R.R. Tolkien and *Beowulf*
Affinities with an ancient poem

As an undergraduate at Exeter College in Oxford, Tolkien explored the Old English poem *Beowulf*, which tells the story of a northern hero whose achievements include slaying a dragon and other supernatural creatures. The historical context for the poem is the sixth century, with it most likely written two centuries later on account of the Christian commentary in the poem, which reflects the success of English Christianity over paganism at that time. This epic story, the first major poem in a vernacular European language, was to become not only a major part of Tolkien's future scholarship, but also a central inspiration for his fiction.

In the poem, the hero Beowulf belongs to a seafaring tribe, the Geats, who live in the south of Sweden, and it recounts two important events in the hero's life. In the first, Beowulf has sailed to the assistance of the Danish king, Hrothgar, whose great hall, Heorot, was being terrorized by the monster Grendel; he slays Grendel and then the fiend's mother, a water-hag, who comes to avenge her son. The second event takes place half a century later: Beowulf has become king of the Geats and reigned for many years when his people are

The Beowulf *manuscript*

attacked by a dragon. As Beowulf fights the monster, both he and the dragon are mortally injured.

During the period when Tolkien was first Reader then Professor of English language at the University of Leeds, he worked on a verse translation of *Beowulf*, which he never completed. He also made a complete prose translation, which as yet lies unpublished in the Bodleian Library Special Collection. Later, Tolkien is likely to have shown or read to his friend C.S. Lewis some of his verse translation of *Beowulf*; he certainly showed Lewis a draft of a prose translation, as the typescript contains amendments in what is more than likely his friend's handwriting.

On 25 November 1936, Tolkien lectured on *Beowulf* to the British Academy in London. The title of his lecture was 'Beowulf: The Monsters and the Critics'. Published in the following year, according to Donald K. Fry, this lecture 'completely altered the course of *Beowulf* studies'. Defending the artistic unity and power of the ancient poem, Tolkien's lecture provides an important key to his work as both a scholar and a writer of fiction.

In his lecture, Tolkien argued that the two monsters that dominate *Beowulf*, Grendel and the dragon, had not been sufficiently considered by scholars as the centre of the poem; Tolkien explained that the poem's theme of monsters actually accounts for its greatness. The life of the piece comes from the quality of its imagination; if a critic over-analyses it, such a vivisection destroys the poem. With great skill, *Beowulf*'s author had created an illusion of historical truth and perspective.

Furthermore, Tolkien argued, in *Beowulf* there is a fusion of the Christian and the ancient north, the old and the new. The author explored insights that may be found in the pagan imagination, which nevertheless point towards the revelations of Christianity. Tolkien concluded his lecture by pointing out: 'In *Beowulf* we have, then, an historical poem about the pagan past, or an attempt at one...It is a poem by a learned man writing of old times, who looking back on the heroism and sorrow feels in them something permanent and something symbolical...He brought probably first to his task a knowledge of Christian poetry...'

Tolkien found a great affinity between his own vision as a writer and that of this ancient poet. For Tolkien, he himself was a Christian storyteller looking back to an imagined northwest European past, his Middle-earth, while the *Beowulf* poet was a Christian looking back at the imaginative resources of a pagan past. Both made use of dragons and other potent symbols, which unified their work; and like the unknown author, Tolkien created an impression of history and a sense of the depths of the past in his stories.

1066 and all that
Reclaiming a lost language and literature

The Norman Conquest is a defining moment in English history, picked up in the title of the still popular parody *1066 and All That* by W.C. Sellar and R.J.Yeatman, now written over 80 years ago. In the early twentieth century, many regarded the Conquest as the origin of modern Britain, with the Anglo-Saxon period before it representing a kind of Dark Age; others saw the Conquest as an act of oppression, in which the indigenous society had been pretty much demolished, thus impoverishing the true culture of England. It is perhaps an exaggeration to say that the Conquest for J.R.R. Tolkien was a matter over which he grieved as if it were a recent traumatic event; however, it did shape both his scholarly work and his creation of Middle-earth.

As a student at St Edward's School in Birmingham, the young Tolkien was introduced to the correct pronunciation of Geoffrey Chaucer's Middle English as a teacher read from *The Canterbury Tales*. He began to recognize the vast changes that had taken place in the English language over the centuries, and started to understand the enormous impact of the Norman Conquest on early English language and literature. For him, London-based Chaucer stood for the establishment of 'modern' Norman and Continental influences against the efforts of other, more conservative, writers who were still

The Norman Conquest depicted in the Bayeux Tapestry

employing older patterns of English from Anglo-Saxon culture; literature after Chaucer was written in a form that resembles more closely modern English. In the event, Tolkien became gripped by the turbulent changes in English language and literature that resulted from the Norman Conquest.

Tolkien believed that, in creating stories like *The Lord of the Rings* and tales about earlier Ages of Middle-earth, he was helping to create a mythology for England. In other words, Tolkien was trying to compensate for the destruction of the rich Old English literature, brought about in large part by the Norman invasion. Surviving texts like *Beowulf* provide a hint of what might have existed; even words and phrases give tantalizing clues to a missing mythology, such as the word 'Earendel' in the text of the old English poem *Christ*. That single name, Tolkien said, helped to inspire his whole mythology of Middle-earth.

In an unfinished story entitled *The Lost Road*, Tolkien supposes that certain Old English words point back to a forgotten language. This is the language of Tolkien's Elvish, which he presented as a discovery rather than something he invented. His mythology of Middle-earth is latent in the Elvish language, he believed.

A talent for acting
*Public recital of Chaucer
from memory*

Although J.R.R. Tolkien did not care for drama, he nevertheless possessed a talent for acting. As a schoolboy, he had performed as the character Mrs Malaprop in Richard Brinsley Sheridan's *The Rivals*; also around that time he wrote and performed in a short play as Christmas entertainment at the home of favourite relatives. In later years, when lecturing on *Beowulf*, he was known to open his presentations with a dramatic recital from the early English text.

In the summers of 1938 and 1939, Tolkien performed in full dress as Geoffrey Chaucer, giving public recitals from memory of stories from *The Canterbury Tales*. In the first year, he recited *The Nun's Priest's Tale*, and in the second, *The Reeve's Tale*. These recitals formed part of the Summer Diversions organized by Nevill Coghill and John Masefield.

Tolkien was greatly inspired by Chaucer's storytelling, and his use of northern dialect in the bawdy *The Reeve's Tale*. Furthermore, he was drawn to Chaucer's evident interest in language, thus writing an important scholarly paper entitled 'Chaucer as Philologist: The Reeve's Tale', based upon a paper he read to the Philological Society in Oxford on 16 May 1931.

Geoffrey Chaucer

J.R.R. Tolkien and Snergs

An unconscious source-book for Hobbits

J.R.R. Tolkien wrote: 'I should like to record my own love and my children's love of E.A. Wyke-Smith's *Marvellous Land of Snergs*, at any rate of the snerg-element of that tale, and of Gorbo the gem of dunderheads, jewel of a companion in an escapade.' Indeed, Tolkien's children liked the story of Snergs so much that they wanted more; the book thus helped to inspire the creation of *The Hobbit*, which started out as bedtime stories told to his youngest sons. Tolkien was later to confess in a letter to the poet W.H. Auden that Wyke-Smith's book may well have been an 'unconscious source-book' for his Hobbit creations.

The land of the Snergs is a 'world apart' to which neglected children rescued by kindly Miss Watkyns and her helpers are taken. Much of the land resembles The Shire, for it is a comfortable, peace-loving place; it is surrounded by a forest inhabited by helpful cinnamon bears. As well as a colony of rescued children at Watkyns

Bay, this land is inhabited by the Snergs, who are 'only slightly taller than the average table but broad in the shoulders and of great strength'. Also in the vicinity is a crew of Dutch sailors, lost for several hundred years, who play a part in the story's happy ending. The land of the Snergs is separated from a wild, dangerous region by a seemingly impassable river banked by sheer cliffs.

In the story two of the children, Sylvia and Joe, decide to visit the town of the Snergs and are joined in their adventure by Gorbo, the 'dunderhead' mentioned by Tolkien. There are touches in the story that have echoes in Tolkien, although the Snergs are clearly the main influence. There is, for example, a door leading into a hidden passage under the river and opened by a spell. Also, the wild land of dangers, with inhabitants such as Mother Meldrum, the wickedest witch, contrasts with the peaceful land of the Snergs. At various points, Sylvia and Joe, along with their companion Gorbo, find themselves in great danger in this region across the river.

The Snergs have a number of Hobbit-like traits, such as a love of eating, feasting at any opportunity, and enjoying company. A direct parallel can be seen between Bilbo Baggins and Gorbo the Snerg, as Gorbo's character develops in response to the challenge of helping Joe and Sylvia in the course of their sometimes perilous adventures.

George MacDonald
An ambivalent influence

The Victorian, Scottish writer George MacDonald was born in Huntly, in rural Aberdeenshire, as the son of a weaver. J.R.R. Tolkien knew

George MacDonald

MacDonald's Curdie stories, *The Princess and the Goblin* and *The Princess and Curdie*, from childhood. Over the years, his attitude to MacDonald became ambivalent, and at times even critical, yet there were many affinities between the two fantasy writers.

In the first instance, the theme of death is central to the fiction of both Tolkien and MacDonald. Moreover, the Scot's thinking about the imagination has some striking similarities with Tolkien's: the goblins in MacDonald's Curdie tales are reminiscent of those in Tolkien's children's story *The Hobbit*, although not as terrifying and utterly malicious as the orcs of *The Lord of the Rings* and *The Silmarillion*. Indeed, Tolkien's shift from naming these creatures 'goblins' to calling them 'orcs' is surely telling. There are hints of a rudimentary invented secondary world in MacDonald's writings; his distinctive Great-Great-grandmother figures have an Elven quality that could belong to Tolkien's world; and he has powerful feminine images of spirituality and providence that are akin to Tolkien's Elf princess Galadriel and to Varda, one of the supreme angelic powers.

Like Tolkien, MacDonald lost his mother in boyhood, a fact that was to influence his thought and writings. He was a close friend of Charles Dodgson – otherwise known as Lewis Carroll – and John Ruskin, the art critic. His insights into the unconscious mind predated the rise of modern psychology and, like Tolkien, he was a literary scholar, although not so distinguished, as well as a storyteller. In places, two key essays entitled 'The imagination: its functions and its culture' (1867) and 'The fantastic imagination' (1882) remarkably foreshadow Tolkien's famed essay 'On fairy-stories'.

When Tolkien, quite late in life, was asked to write a preface to an edition of Macdonald's *The Golden Key*, the process clarified for him his disquiet with some of Macdonald's fairy tales. Instead of completing this preface, he ended up writing his story *Smith of Wootton Major*, which profoundly explores how glimpses of other worlds transform art and craft in human life. This was to be his last story.

GOBLINS UNDER THE MOUNTAINS

Tolkien acknowledged that George MacDonald's were among the stories that influenced the 'background' of his imagination from the time of his childhood. In MacDonald's **The Princess and the Goblin,** *a boy miner named Curdie is aware of the goblins that are rife in the mountain tunnels he knows. Tolkien made it clear that he owed a debt to MacDonald's 'classic' goblins in his own portrayal of them in* **The Hobbit.**

Ancient riddles
Sources of Bilbo and Gollum's contest

A dramatic sequence in *The Hobbit* is the life-and-death exchange of riddles between Bilbo Baggins and Gollum. Their shared knowledge of the tradition of riddles is a hint at Gollum's ancestry; he was once a Hobbit in the days before the race migrated westwards over the Misty Mountains to what became The Shire.

The various riddles used by Gollum and Bilbo are examples of a number, some more obvious than others, which J.R.R. Tolkien employs in both *The Hobbit* and *The Lord of the Rings*. By doing so, he was drawing on an important feature of Old English and Old Norse poetry, more recent literature including Shakespeare, and even children's nursery rhymes.

One repository of riddles is the Old English *Exeter Book*, which has more than 90. These vary in length and cover a wide range of subjects, both secular and religious. It is probable that they were written down in the eight century AD and reflect the culture of England before the Norman Conquest, just as those bandied between Bilbo and

Gollum often reflect Hobbit life. One describes a bookworm – a literal one devouring a book's parchment pages, not an avid reader – that concludes, 'The thievish visitant was no whit the wiser for swallowing the words' (R.K. Gordon's translation). Riddle contests like the one between Gollum and Bilbo can be found in Old Norse literature that would have been familiar to Tolkien, such as the *Elder Edda*.

Bookworm damage

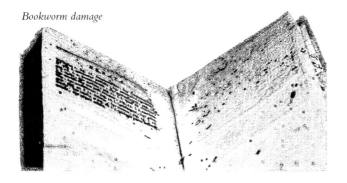

J.R.R. TOLKIEN BIBLIOGRAPHY

A Middle English Vocabulary. The Clarendon Press: Oxford, 1922. Prepared for use with Kenneth Sisam's *Fourteenth Century Verse and Prose* (The Clarendon Press: Oxford, 1921) and later published with it.

Sir Gawain and the Green Knight. Edited by J.R.R. Tolkien and E.V. Gordon. The Clarendon Press: Oxford, 1925 (new edition, revised by Norman Davis, 1967).

The Hobbit, or There and Back Again. George Allen and Unwin: London, 1937.

Farmer Giles of Ham. George Allen and Unwin: London, 1950.

The Fellowship of the Ring: Being the First Part of The Lord of the Rings. George Allen and Unwin: London, 1954.

The Two Towers: Being the Second Part of The Lord of the Rings. George Allen and Unwin: London, 1954.

The Return of the King: Being the Third Part of The Lord of the Rings. George Allen and Unwin: London, 1955.

The Adventures of Tom Bombadil and Other Verses From The Red Book. George Allen and Unwin: London, 1962.

Ancrene Wisse: The English Text of the Ancrene Riwle. Edited by J.R.R. Tolkien. Oxford University Press: London, 1962.

Tree and Leaf. George Allen and Unwin: London, 1964.

The Tolkien Reader. Ballantine Books: New York, 1966.

The Road Goes Ever On: A Song Cycle. Poems by J.R.R. Tolkien, music by Donald Swann. George Allen and Unwin: London, 1968. (Enlarged edition, 1978.)

Smith of Wootton Major. George Allen and Unwin: London, 1967.

POSTHUMOUS WRITINGS

Sir Gawain and the Green Knight, Pearl and Sir Orfeo. Translated by J. R. R. Tolkien; edited by Christopher Tolkien. George Allen and Unwin: London, 1975.

The Father Christmas Letters. Edited by Baillie Tolkien. George Allen and Unwin: London, 1976.

The Silmarillion. Edited by Christopher Tolkien. George Allen and Unwin: London, 1977. *Pictures by J.R.R. Tolkien.* Edited by Christopher Tolkien. George Allen and Unwin: London, 1979.

Unfinished Tales of Numenor and Middle-earth. Edited by Christopher Tolkien. George Allen and Unwin: London, 1980.

The Letters of J.R.R. Tolkien. Edited by Humphrey Carpenter, with the assistance of Christopher Tolkien. George Allen and Unwin: London, 1981.

Old English Exodus. Text, translation and commentary by J.R.R. Tolkien; edited by Joan Turville-Petre. The Clarendon Press: Oxford, 1981.

Finn and Hengest: The Fragment and the Episode. Edited by Alan Bliss. George Allen and Unwin: London, 1982.

Mr Bliss. George Allen and Unwin: London, 1982.

The Monsters and the Critics and Other Essays. Edited by Christopher Tolkien. George Allen and Unwin: London, 1983.

The History of Middle-earth. Edited by Christopher Tolkien. Published in twelve volumes between 1983 and 1994, by George Allen and Unwin, Unwin Hyman and HarperCollins.

Roverandom. Edited by Christina Scull and Wayne G. Hammond. HarperCollins: London, 1998.

The Children of Húrin. Edited by Christopher Tolkien. HarperCollins: London, 2007.

The Legend of Sigurd and Gudrún. Edited by Christopher Tolkien. HarperCollins: London, 2009.

PICTURE CREDITS

King Edward's School: Robert Kirkup Dent
The real Bag End: Colin Duriez
The ring: Lucy Davey
W.H. Auden: Carl Van Vechten

These files are licensed under the Creative Commons Attribution 2.0 Generic license:
Bletchley Park: Draco2008
Aftermath of the storm, 1987: David Wright

These files are licensed under the terms of the GNU Free Documentation License, Version 1.2:
Waterworks, Edgbaston: Oosoom
Sarehole Mill: Oosoom
Solar barge of Khufu: Berthold Werner

These files are licensed under the Creative Commons Attribution-Share Alike 3.0 Unported license:
The plough: http://en.wikipedia.org/wiki/User:B00P & me (SAE1962 10:04, 2 April 2008 (UTC))
Jungfrau: Earth explorer
Warwick Castle: Mcselede
Wayland's Smithy: Author unknown
The grave of J.R.R. and Edith Tolkien: Stefan Servos
The Sindarin word "gwilwileth": Olaf Studt – Hämbörger
Pauline Baynes: Luis Segovia
Viggo Mortensen: Angela George
Gothmog, Lord of the Balrogs, riding a dragon: Tttom
Treebeard, the Ent: TTThom
Eagle: Juan lacruz
Spider: Acrocynus
Exeter College, Oxford: Exet

The Eagle and Child in St Giles, Oxford: Tom Murphy VII
Leonard Nimroy: Gage Skidmore
BBC Microphone: Alvar_Lidell.jpg: Liftarn
St Johns Ashfield Stained Glass Good Shepherd: Alfred Handel, d. 1946, photo:Toby Hudson
Bookworm damage: Ragesoss

These files are licensed under the Creative Commons Attribution-Share Alike 2.0 Generic license:
Lydney Park: Jeff Collins
Sir Ian McKellen: Southbanksteve
St Peter and St Paul's Church, Worminghall: Steve Daniels
The Great Hall, University of Leeds: Betty Longbottom
Statue of C. S. Lewis: Genvessel

These files are licensed under the Creative Commons Attribution-Share Alike 2.5 Generic license:
Addison's Walk at Magdalen College, Oxford: Original Gagravarr
St Aloysius's Roman Catholic Church: Kaihsu Tai.

INDEX

MORE AMAZING TITLES

LOVED THIS BOOK?

Tell us what you think and you could win another fantastic book from David & Charles in our monthly prize draw.

www.lovethisbook.co.uk

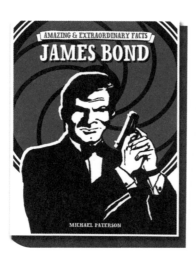

AMAZING & EXTRAORDINARY FACTS: JAMES BOND
Michael Paterson
ISBN: 978-1-4463-0195-1

The essential companion for every Bond fan, unearthing a selection of surprising and intruiging facts about the much-loved fictional spy, and the books and films that he has starred in. It is brimming with strange and amusing stories about the Bond actors, from Sean Connery to Daniel Craig, behind the scenes at the film set, and amazing facts about Ian Fleming's original novels.

AMAZING & EXTRAORDINARY FACTS: LONDON
Stephen Halliday
ISBN: 978-0-7153-3910-7

A unique collection of strange laws, heroic deeds, surprising revelations and other quirky stories that have shaped the unique history of Britain's capital. London's long history is an extraordinarily rich source of amazing facts, whether your interest is political, social, architectural or historical, you will find a variety of topics in this alternative guide to London.

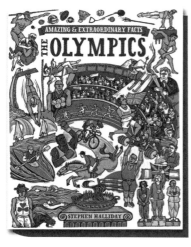

AMAZING & EXTRAORDINARY FACTS: THE OLYMPICS
Stephen Halliday
ISBN: 978-1-4463-0201-9

A unique and entertaining collection of facts surrounding the Olympic Games. From their origins in ancient Greece to the most famous Olympic medalists, the book covers a range of fascinating trivia for every sport lover to enjoy. You can discover the athletes who have set the marks for modern sporting excellence, and wonder at the records set by competitors across the years.

A DAVID & CHARLES BOOK
F&W Media International, Ltd 2012

David & Charles is an imprint of F&W Media International, Ltd
Brunel House, Forde Close, Newton Abbot, TQ12 4PU, UK

F&W Media International, Ltd is a subsidiary of F+W Media, Inc
10151 Carver Road, Suite #200, Blue Ash, OH 45242, USA

Text © Colin Duriez 2012
Layout © F&W Media International, Ltd 2012

First published in the UK and USA in 2012

Colin Duriez has asserted his right to be identified as author of this work in accordance with
the Copyright, Designs and Patents Act, 1988.

All rights reserved. No part of this publication may be reproduced in any form or by any
means, electronic or mechanical, by photocopying, recording or otherwise, without prior
permission in writing from the publisher.

A catalogue record for this book is available from the British Library.

ISBN-13: 978-1-4463-0269-9 hardback
ISBN-10: 1-4463-0269-5 hardback

Printed in China by Toppan Leefung Printing Limited for:
F&W Media International, Ltd
Brunel House, Forde Close, Newton Abbot, TQ12 4PU, UK

10 9 8 7 6 5 4 3 2 1

Junior Acquisitions Editor: Verity Graves-Morris
Project Editor: Freya Dangerfield
Design Manager Sarah Clark
Production Manager: Beverley Richardson

F+W Media publishes high quality books on a wide range of subjects.
For more great book ideas visit: www.fwmedia.co.uk